EXTREME ENTREPRENEUR

Mark Baven

A Lark Production

Entrepreneur Press

Managing Editor: Marla Markman
Cover Design: Mark Kozak
Composition and production: Eliot House Productions

This publication is designed to provide accurate and authoritative information in
regard to the subject matter covered. It is sold with the understanding that the publisher is not engaged in rendering legal, accounting or other professional services. If
legal advice or other expert assistance is required, the services of a competent professional person should be sought.

Library of Congress Cataloging-in-Publication Data
Baven, Mark.
    Extreme entrepreneur : on the edge / Mark Baven.
    p. cm.
    ISBN 1-891984-19-5
    1. Entrepreneurship. 2 Businesspeople. I. Title.
HB615 .B4 2001
658.4'21--dc21   2001023080

Printed in Canada

09 08 07 06 05 04 03 02 01 . . . . .10 9 8 7 6 5 4 3 2 1

Contents

Part III

EXTREME SIZZLE AND SALES

Acknowledgments

I would like to thank Don Logay for his contribution.

Preface

t's only appropriate to begin this book with a look at extreme entrepreneurs' (EEs) aspirations beyond their business spheres. In fact, the visionary quality is the great EE unifier. The theme threads through all the succeeding chapters and topics—and forms the common link among all the individuals discussed or mentioned in this book.

In all their endeavors, the extremists see possibilities that "mere mortals" fail to notice or can't summon up the combination of nerve, confidence, and determination to tackle. From breakthrough selling propositions, to maverick marketing maneuvers, larger-than-life image conjurings, and sales manifestos, extreme entrepreneurs seem to follow road signs on routes no one else can fathom.

The entrepreneurs described in these pages are a representative sample, not a comprehensive catalog. There are countless other EEs that would merit inclusion, many just as amazing (or more so) as the ones covered herein. Several who come to mind are:

- Patagonia founder Yvon Chouinard, who spawned the high-perform-ance sports equipment and clothing industry as an offshoot of his unprecedented extreme outdoor sports pursuits, and runs his company along rigorously environmental lines.
- Rock impressario Bill Graham, who fled the Holocaust and on these shores created and built the rock concert industry, a radically new par-adigm of art performance that has generated many billions of dollars in revenue.
- A.P. Giannini, the immigrant's son who invented the branch bank con-cept and transformed banking from an elitist privilege to a populist right.

This book could easily be twice as long. But the point was not to be exhaustive, but to inspire, to offer a different lens to view entrepreneurial endeavors—and to perceive business possibilities. Above all, it serves as a reminder that if you actively look for something you haven't seen before, you just might find it.

part

IN EXTREMIS

If you could imagine an organization—a club, if you will—of extreme entrepreneurs, what do you think its motto would be? *Damn the torpedoes, full speed ahead? Live free or die?* Or *last one in is a rotten egg?*

It'd probably be some combination of all three, and the club itself would be filled with a wacky, mixed bag of entrepreneurs ranging from Howard Hughes to Marc Andreeson to Oprah Winfrey. The club meetings would feel like a room full of lightbulbs going off and on and it would likely be difficult to get a word in edgewise.

The point is, each of the extreme entrepreneurs that will turn up in the pages that follow couldn't be more different from the other, but they are, all together, in a league of their own. They share qualities, experiences, and accomplishments that are unique and just plain different from the rest of the world. And they'd probably agree that being extreme is a state of mind, or a state out of mind, as the case may be, a chronic case of *in extremis*.

A BREED
Apart

Discussions about the nature of the "entrepreneurial personality" have been rife for most of the past century, mainly focusing on the born-versus-made debate. After a hundred years or so of observing the extraordinary entrepreneurial achievements of so many, it's safe to say that there are some true naturals. But most entrepreneurs just plain work hard at it, and proper mentoring and instruction go a long way in helping entrepreneurs develop their edge and avoid judgment blunders.

While people can enhance their measure of the qualities that contribute to entrepreneurial success, these personality traits still aren't evenly distributed among the population. Some people flat out will never be entrepreneurs, while others will have to struggle to make even a modest go of it, and still others will perform off the charts. Generally speaking, extreme entrepreneurs (EEs) are among the most naturally inclined and well-suited for the entrepreneurial life—these are the ones who are off the charts.

1

chapter

So, to an extent, it's true to say EEs are just like other entrepreneurs—only more so. Entrepreneurs by definition are risk-takers—they're taking a personal risk just by putting up the shingle. Extreme entrepreneurs actively court the do-or-die situations. Others in business may be driven, but EEs are *obsessed*. While most entrepreneurs can adequately cope with failure, EEs snort in its general direction. They don't push the envelope; they incinerate it.

But the perspective just described is, ultimately, an oversimplification, useful to describe the shape of the forest but of little value in identifying the trees. EEs are at least as complex as any other group of people, so they don't easily submit to such typecasting. It's hard to avoid some icon worship when it comes to extremely successful and wealthy business leaders, but we need to remember these are mere mortals, after all, just as prone to human foibles as anyone else.

Like any group of highly creative people, extreme entrepreneurs exhibit a huge range of characteristics. This chapter looks at some traits that seem especially characteristic of EEs. Some traits apply across the board (e.g., virtually all EEs are driven) while others are present only selectively. The combination of traits and tendencies in an EE such as Netscape's Jim Clark, for example, isn't discernible in Ted Turner. The motivations and gratifications of, say, Andrew Carnegie, who had a passion for travel and culture, were hardly echoed by the likes of, say, Sam Walton. They're each a different species of bird, but they are all birds.

The Basics

The basic attributes common among virtually all extreme entrepreneurs revolve around desire and persistence. This is meant to cover the battery of rough synonyms, such as "conviction" and "intensity." But this core set of qualities is mandatory. There are no accidental extreme entrepreneurs. There are no reluctant EEs either. They're out there because they want to be and because they mean to be. The word "hellbent" comes to mind. The following are some of the basics among the extreme:

Enterprise

This energetic, resourceful quality kicks in early. The kid who opens his or her own lemonade stand is an icon of American lore, and indeed

EE Superstar: Ted Turner

Some EEs come charging out the gate of adolescence full bore, with total confidence they'll create the destinations to suit themselves. Media tycoon Ted Turner is a prime example.

Preternaturally charming and bright, the 24-year-old Atlantan inherited the family billboard business in 1963, after his father committed suicide. No one should misconstrue this "gift" as a stacked deck. For starters, the company was near ruin. Turner's first order of business was to follow through on a takeover deal his father had set up but then desperately tried to void. By running up a string of acquisitions, within five years Turner had parlayed his inheritance into the dominant outdoor advertising company in the South.

His next step was to buy a small radio station. Partly by working the synergy between the media he controlled, Turner was able to buy more stations. He made the logical jump into television in 1970. But he had no understanding of the medium, and what he'd acquired was a sub-piffling station that barely flickered its way into a few hundred homes on the clearest of days.

> Whatever and whoever he's impelled to take on next, Turner remains one of the most colorful and authentic EEs of the past several decades.

Bold to the point of recklessness (or so his associates thought), Turner put everything on the line, as he would again and again. He bought a satellite uplink to take advantage of the revolutionary new cable-TV technology and leapt into national exposure. Turner decided to push baseball coverage, and to secure that niche he bought the Atlanta Braves. (Buying a sports team appears to be an elite EE ritual, from William Wrigley, Jr., to Wayne Huizenga.)

Turner was most prescient in his certainty that an all-news cable station was inevitable. Determined to be the one to get there first, he launched the Cable News Network. Once again, he did so by putting everything on the line—to the tune of $100 million, most of it in the form of debt. Over time, Turner grew CNN into the presiding live visual news source, and eventually sold it to Time-Warner in a multi-billion dollar deal. Whatever and whoever he's impelled to take on next, Turner remains one of the most colorful and authentic EEs of the past several decades.

many EEs did show signs of commercial exuberance from the get-go. The child who thought to charge schoolmates to see an appendectomy scar was certainly more likely to be looking an extreme entrepreneur in the mirror years later. This venturesome tendency only becomes more so over time.

The Pennsylvania-born son of a German brickmaker, Henry J. Heinz started to bottle and sell his own horseradish as a teenager, and used the profits to buy a half interest in his father's business. A few years later, his father returned from a trip to Germany to find his son had built a grand new home during his absence—paid for by collections of debts that the older man had written off.

William Wrigley, Jr., ran away from home the summer of his 11th year, not because of family problems (things were fine at home), but because he had a need to take his measure against the world. Once he made his way to New York City, Wrigley got a job as a newspaper boy and slept on top of sidewalk gratings. He stayed in touch with his parents back in Philadelphia via postcard, and returned home when the adventure had run its course, in time to resume school in the fall and far more confident in his capacities.

Michael Rubin, founder and CEO of Global Sports Inc., was a notorious junior extreme entrepreneur. Before he cracked 30, he'd already launched a dozen or more ventures since his first at the age of eight. His entrepreneurial exploits had landed him on the pages of *The Wall Street Journal*, *USA Today*, and *People*—all before his feet had stopped growing! Now at the helm of GSI, a multi-million dollar developer and operator of e-commerce sporting goods businesses, Rubin is unlikely to have landed on his last entrepreneurial endeavor. Once an extreme entrepreneur, ever an EE.

> Once an extreme entrepreneur, ever an EE.

Determination

This is the über-quality that every extreme entrepreneur possesses: tremendous energy and force of will in pursuing goals. Examples are as numerous as EEs themselves. Mary Kay Ash, for example, has always been unswervably focused; when she was plying products for Stanley Home Products, a company convention inspired her to shoot for the following year's sales crown. She set up three or four two-hour product parties a day, seven days a week, for the next year, and indeed she snagged the top honor at the next convocation. She brought this quality to bear on everything she attempted, and built a vast direct-sales empire as a result.

EEs face adversity with equanimity, and show astonishing resilience and determination in their capacity to rebound. When Heinz' first venture flopped disastrously, enraged creditors had him arrested for fraud—twice. He was absolved both times, and it took him all of a year to launch his next company, in 1876, with $3,000 borrowed from his family. This time he proceeded with more fiscal prudence, but he took a most free-wheeling approach to promotion, deploying every trick around and inventing a few of his own. H.J. Heinz Co. survives to this day.

> EEs face adversity with equanimity, and show astonishing resilience and determination in their capacity to rebound.

Trammell Crow is the founder of one of the largest commercial real estate dynasties in U.S. history. Son of a humble Dallas bookkeeper, Crow grew up during the depression and adopted an innovative approach to real estate. Instead of looking to sell properties and take the depreciation as profit, Crow's concept was to hold on to his properties and leverage them for all they were worth. His stock phrase was, "You can get rich selling real estate, but you can only get wealthy owning it." Crow was known as one of the world's most optimistic souls, but most associates, friends, journalists, and analysts attributed Crow's astounding success to his creativity, incredible energy, and—above all—willpower. As one of Crow's partners said of him in *Inc.* magazine, "The real secret of Trammell Crow is that he works harder than you do. He believes that persistence is far more important than genius. Never, never, *NEVER* give up—that's his motto."

Work-Centrism

Calling an EE a workaholic is a bit unfair. It is like calling a general a "control freak." EEs are similar to artists in their obsession with their work, their tendency to lose themselves in the flow, and their monomaniacal drive to do one thing extraordinarily well. For many of them, life is work and work is life and the lack of a clear line between the two is just fine by them.

Retiring to Southern California in 1967 after selling his (second) namesake company, 65-year-old aviation pioneer William P. Lear became dejected, nearly moribund. Rather than yielding to disintegration and death, however, Lear relocated. He took his fourth wife and their youngest child to Reno, Nevada, where he established a laboratory to work on a new dream—an efficient steam engine for automobiles. When this experiment failed to pan out, he resumed work on improving the small commercial jets he'd developed at Lear Jet Inc. He lived until the age of 76, in full vigor, remaining at his shop until a few days before his death from leukemia.

Frederick Henry Royce was even more extreme. He would become so engrossed in trying to perfect an element of his car—which was already acknowledged to be the world's best-engineered—worried staff members would have to cajole Royce into eating. His death, at the age of 70, was said to be the result of overwork.

MCI founder William McGowan and financier John Bogle both kept on working after they had heart transplants. Somehow the word "workaholic" doesn't do justice to such behavior.

Risk-Seeking

In the popular view, entrepreneurs tend to be risk lovers; after all, roughly 40 percent of all businesses (depending on statistical sources) fail within the first two years, making entrepreneurship one of the most inherently risky career choices. By such reasoning, EEs would be veritable Evel Knievels of the business world. The extreme entrepreneur is a risk magnet and a riskmaster. They may not always love the risk, but they sure know how to work with it.

> The extreme entrepreneur is a risk magnet and a riskmaster.

Walt Disney, for example, was known to put everything he had on the line for the next project. According to legend, FedEx's Fred Smith once took the last of FedEx's funds to Vegas and ran it on craps to win enough to cover payroll. (Supposedly, he succeeded.) Ted Turner is known for risking to the hilt every time he moved on to a new iteration in business. Not all EEs are so hard core, but many approach risk with an attitude somewhere between brazen disregard and taunting confrontation.

C|Net is a high-profile company that delivers news and information about technology through online services and television. CEO and founder Halsey Minor has faced his share of obstacles on the road to success. Though his company is currently valued at more than $3 billion, there was a moment in 1994 when it looked like the fat lady might sing. An entrepreneur with less of a stomach for the massive risk Minor was taking would have looked for the exit sign. Not Minor. The greater the risk, the greater the stakes, and the greater his determination to make good. Minor himself has said of his roughest days, "I could go bankrupt, but I was not going to quit." Clearly, this is an extreme entrepreneur with an iron stomach for risk.

The Contrarian

Everyone knows hard-core entrepreneurs are industrial-strength Type A's. They are rarely the ones known for going with the flow—going against the grain is more like it. They don't rock the boat to rock the boat, but it's often their nature to shake things up to make room for their particular innovation.

Insurance industry maverick Bob MacDonald is just such an iconoclast. In the early 1980s, he led a public campaign against the insurance industry's most popular sort of policy—whole life—and was denounced by everyone in the business. Knowing the innovations he believed would save his industry would never happen within the mainstream, he launched LifeUSA, a company he imagined could be the FedEx or Wal-Mart of the insurance industry. Indeed, by flying in the face of conventional wisdom, and embracing his role as contrarian, he's changed the rules of the insurance game.

> They are rarely the ones known for going with the flow—going against the grain is more like it.

A notorious boat rocker, MacDonald has said, "I've never been comfortable as part of a crowd." Good thing, too: LifeUSA turned the tide in insurance by inventing products that insure people against living too long rather than dying young. German insurance giant Allianz acquired MacDonald's LifeUSA for $540 million in 1999.

Charisma

Among the defining characteristics of an extreme entrepreneur, personal magnetism ranks high. A partial source is the sheer power of conviction. The absolute commitment to product and company is itself galvanizing. It is difficult to refuse or ignore someone who is completely sure of his or her vision. So EEs frequently are superb persuaders—winning over tough sales targets, executive prospects, or reluctant bankers. Also, successful, high-achieving people tend to amass an ineffable gravity that others pick up on right away. Those used to being heeded and taken seriously project that expectation.

> Among the defining characteristics of an extreme entrepreneur, personal magnetism ranks high.

EEs also tend to be naturally endowed with that compelling *something* that makes certain people captivating on stage, in social settings, or at business meetings. As someone once said of a renowned scholar and teacher, "Wherever he sat, that was the head of the table."

Mary Kay Ash is charisma personified. Her ability to whip a crowd of sales associates into hypermotivated frenzy has been her not-so-secret weapon. Associates cite Kay's epic exhortations, even ahead of the trademark bonus awards (the famed top rung being a pink Cadillac), as the force that inspires them when times are rough.

"Personality" EEs such as Oprah Winfrey trade almost exclusively on their charisma. Oprah's ultimate "product" is her captivating personality, and the trust it engenders in millions of TV spectators. Among her many other accomplishments, it is her sincerity, enthusiasm, and humor that have single-handedly driven a resurgence in middlebrow literature sales, with her own Barnes & Noble shelf to prove it.

Charisma makes for good copy, and good copy drives impressive sales. Extreme entrepreneurs such as Richard Branson, Ted Turner, and Herb Kelleher project a quality of self-delight that the public can revel in, and which creates a momentum quite distinct from the business itself.

Going Places

In the same way the savvy investor scans the horizon looking for the next hot stock pick, biz hounds are always looking for the next extreme

EE Drop Outs (& Booted-Outs)

A lot of extreme entrepreneurs didn't finish their schooling: Sometimes because family poverty dictated that they had to begin earning at a young age. Sometimes it was their rebellious streak manifesting itself. And sometimes they were just eager to get their entrepreneurial show on the road. EEs aren't averse to education, but they are often sufficiently aware of their own will and vision that education as an end rather than a means makes little sense. It's easy to see how school might drop off the immediate agenda when a real-life entrepreneurial opportunity knocks.

Soichiro Honda was an EE with an attitude when it came to education. "I didn't want a diploma," he said. "They had less value than a cinema ticket. A ticket at least guaranteed that you would get in. A diploma guaranteed nothing."

Here's the educational rap sheet on some interesting EEs:

- Bill Bartmann (founder, Commercial Finance Services)—high school dropout
- Richard Branson—left school at 16
- Bill Gates—dropped out of Harvard
- Henry J. Heinz—finished his schooling at 14
- Soichiro Honda—dropped out of technical high school
- Howard Hughes—left college
- Wayne Huizenga—college dropout
- Steven Jobs—dropped out of college
- Mitch Kapor (Lotus)—dropped out of business school
- Ray Kroc (McDonald's)—grade school dropout
- William P. Lear (Lear, Inc., & Lear Jet, Inc.)—eighth-grade dropout
- Jeno Paulucci (Chun King Corp., Jeno's Inc., and Luigino's Inc.)—dropped out of college
- Helena Rubinstein—dropped out of technical school
- Harland Sanders (Kentucky Fried Chicken)— grade school dropout
- Jack Stack (Springfield ReManufacturing Corp.)—thrown out of college and a Catholic seminary
- Cornelius Vanderbilt—no schooling at all
- Ted Waitt (Gateway 2000)—dropped out of college

> EEs aren't averse to education, but they are often sufficiently aware of their own will and vision that education as an end rather than a means rarely makes sense.

> The
> attributes of the
> extreme entrepreneur
> attract outside enthusi-
> asm in critical forms:
> financing, employees,
> customers, and
> media attention.

entrepreneur. Why? The EEs are where the action is (or where it's going to be) and profit is sure to follow. The qualities described above are compelling, especially to those who don't share them. Non-EEs want to warm their hands by the glow of the passion the EE possesses.

The attributes of the extreme entrepreneur attract outside enthusiasm in critical forms: financing, employees, customers, and media attention. In other words, the extreme qualities create the kind of momentum the average entrepreneur might not experience in a lifetime.

True Globalism

When discussing the package of entrepreneurial traits, remember that our own cultural biases shape our thinking. America is the world leader in entrepreneurship, but there have been plenty of outstanding European and Asian entrepreneurs as well, and their attributes don't necessarily conform to our vision of the EE. We tend to put a premium on "positive" aggressive traits, and envision the ideal entrepreneur as a cross between Rambo and Vince Lombardi. But elsewhere, especially in Asia, cultural history has produced a very different breed.

N.R. Narayana Murthy, who founded Infosys Technologies Ltd. in 1981, is India's leading software tycoon. Though he's worth well over a half-billion dollars, Murthy still starts the day by cleaning his family's toilet and attending to other small domestic chores. Inspired by India's long tradition of ascetic visionaries, the technology mogul is humble, nearly to the point of self-effacement. Murthy is an avid champion of "compassionate capitalism" as the best approach to alleviate India's brutal poverty. For him, the phrase is not rhetoric, but a philosophy that balances personal gain against the greater good. And he has molded his corporation in accordance with his vision.

Then there's Japan's telecommunications giant Kazuo Inamori, one of the most extraordinary EEs alive. Inamori founded Kyocera Corporation

Extreme Entrepreneur

12

in 1959 and guided its evolution into a multi-billion dollar player in a huge sweep of cutting-edge technologies internationally. In 1984, he formed both DDI Corp. (in cooperation with 23 other companies) and the philanthropic Inamori Foundation. Since then, he's created another five corporations. Inamori's companies generate tens of billions of dollars in annual sales, and he's been a key architect in Japan's wireless communication upsurge.

Inamori lives by and propounds a philosophical doctrine based on the motto, "respect the divine and love people." He believes a business leader must balance the twin extremes of boldness and prudence. According to Inamori, those blessed with innate gifts must be humble in appreciation of their good fortune, even as they make best use of these talents. He warns high-achieving entrepreneurs to beware of surrounding themselves with flatterers, as such praise can sap their energy and integrity. Inamori applies a simple formula to gauge the success quotient of an individual's life—ability (0 – 100) x enthusiasm (0 – 100) x attitude—which, significantly, can range from –100 to +100.

Gotta Have It

Extreme entrepreneurs are the "It Girls" (1920s term referring to the hot, popular presonality of the moment) of the biz world. So what adds up to "it?" According to Michael Phillips and Salli Rasberry, who defined the concept in *Honest Business*, and to Paul Hawken, who refined it in *Growing a Business*, "it" is your *trade-skill*, a cluster of crucial attributes for successful entrepreneurship. Based on their own experiences (Phillips developed MasterCard, Rasberry is a business consultant, and Hawken is a serial entrepreneur and business visionary), the authors urge aspiring entrepreneurs to *realistically* appraise their trade-skills. Deficiency in one or more of the traits may indicate you're not suited for entrepreneurship. In that case, one possible solution is to partner with someone whose strengths compensate for your shortfalls.

The five traits are as follows:

1. *Persistence*. This means sticking with the program even after your enthusiasm has waned. It also means following through on all the mundane, unglamorous, tedious tasks necessary to cultivate and sustain a business.
2. *Ability to face facts*. This refers to a capacity to react to the real situation rather than your fantasies or sense of what "should" be correct. Belief

systems, habitual perceptions, and other forms of conditioning can badly skew decision-making. Facing the facts means letting go of such filters when the evidence warrants.

3. *Ability to minimize risks.* This means choosing a lower-risk, lower-payoff option over a high-risk, windfall proposition. Since there's plenty of risk inherent in business ventures, savvy entrepreneurs, according to the authors, make sure to have fallback plans, alternative solutions, and cutoff points. It could be said that EEs tend to evince less of this trait than the common run of entrepreneurs, or at least they have the gift of managing their extreme risk, rather than minimizing it.

4. *Being a hands-on learner.* Delegating is critical, of course, but strong entrepreneurs actively examine every element of their business, whether it's the fine print of a contract, new technology, ad copy, or new office wiring. This means being a detail person who needs empirical confirmation to establish confidence. It is not synonymous with micro-managing, but that is the obvious too-much-of-a-good-thing danger—especially during the transition from an entrepreneurial company to a managerial one.

5. *Ability to grasp numbers.* This is an intuitive sense of numeral logic, not the capacity to analyze a monthly profit-loss statement. Numbers express relationships that partially dictate an entrepreneur's course. Someone who needs to take time to recalculate in the face of every business order or expenditure is likely to have trouble sustaining a big-picture-based action plan.

Trade-skill is a powerful conceptual tool for gauging one's own level of preparedness. But as with any set of rules, its terms are not inviolable nor should anyone take them as absolute. For starters, the rules are better suited to regular entrepreneurs than to EEs; if all fledgling EEs were to "face facts," most business breakthroughs would never have come to pass. A recurrent theme among EEs is that they were too foolish and uninformed to realize how impossible a goal they'd set. Hugh Hefner probably put it best: "I was the ultimate double threat: broke and inexperienced." Without a certain measure of self-delusion, entrepreneurs couldn't dare to dream. When EEs discuss their achievements, a majority of them emphasize that what the world saw as risky, they saw as inevitable, obvious.

RULEBREAKERS
and
Trendbuckers

B eing an entrepreneur is risky business. Every entrepreneurial business—from the corner mom-and-pop deli to the cutting-edge dotcom—is inherently risky. But there are degrees of risk, and some entrepreneurs—the extreme entrepreneurs—are willing to go as far out on a limb as they possibly can to make a go of a good idea. So how do you know an extreme entrepreneur when you see one?

For starters, the entrepreneur usually has the maniacal gleam in his or her eye. The EE is also the rulebreaker, the out-of-the-box thinker, and the unconventional operator. An EE has a spectacular, gigantic vision, and pedal-to-the-medal drive to match.

It's easy to scan the entrepreneurial horizon and see the high-profile, head-and-shoulders-above-the-others entrepreneurs who have made their extreme marks. The Henry Fords and the Sam Waltons and the Bill Gateses. You can learn a lot from these giants, to be sure, but you can learn just as much from the extreme

2

folks whose names you don't recognize, the clever entrepreneurs who are forging their big visions in their various small corners of the business world.

Extremities in All Directions

The extreme entrepreneurs have been the prime agents of change in every facet of business, such as:

○ *Products*. The extreme entrepreneurs almost always invent the best new stuff. Dr. Edwin Land pitched his idea for an instant camera to his employer, but Kodak founder George Eastman just couldn't see it. So Land decided to launch his own company, Polaroid Corporation, in 1937. Snap that, Mr. Eastman!

○ *Services*. The extreme entrepreneurs come up with ideas for services we didn't even know we needed. In a famous anecdote, Fred Smith's business-school professor scoffed at his student's idea for an overnight delivery business. FedEx is the "implausible" outcome of Smith's brainstorm, and that teacher must feel like the record executive who dismissed the Beatles demo with an offhand, "no commercial potential."

○ *Company management*. Extreme entrepreneurs often run their operations in innovative ways that push their ventures to extraordinary levels. While Herb Kelleher's Southwest Airlines is renowned for many virtues—such as reliability, no-frills budget fares, and excellent rapport between staff and passengers—he considers the single most critical factor in the airline's phenomenal success story to be the exceptional treatment of its work force. Kelleher insists on maintaining a superb flow of communication, extraordinarily positive work environment, and accordance of great respect and responsibility to all Southwest employees. Kelleher's management philosophy emphasizes the continuum between management, workers, and customers, rather than focusing solely on the employee/client interface. One could argue that without Kelleher's bold and unusual approach to management, Southwest Airlines would be just another airline. In the extreme, management matters.

○ *Business models*. The extreme entrepreneur has been known to take traditional business models and turn them on their ear. Take Bill Gross and his idealab!, which represents a thoroughly modern, brand-spanking new business model—the "start-up factory" that is part think tank, part venture capitalist, part business incubator, and part parent company.

Instead of seeking to centralize control, idealab!'s premise is to spin off authority. Gross creates and organizes small companies—and once one proves viable, he allows its executives to find their own flight path. His brood includes CitySearch (city guides with local content), PayMyBills.com (consumer bill-paying service), GoTo.com (Web site locator), and PeopleLink (outsourced provider of community solutions for the Internet). Gross, who describes himself as an incurable entrepreneur, has created an entity that seeks to combine the advantageous resources of a large company with the agility of a small one.

○ *Manufacturing*. Besides dreaming up new stuff to make, extreme entrepreneurs are often at the forefront of new ways of making the stuff. Henry Ford is usually seen as *the* ultimate exemplar of American entrepreneurship in this regard. He is generally accorded the lion's share of the credit for his company's manufacturing innovations, starting with the assembly line.

> Besides dreaming up new stuff to make, extreme entrepreneurs are often at the fore-front of new ways of making the stuff.

○ *Distribution*. Sometimes the extreme entrepreneur is responsible for figuring out the new ways to get the stuff to where the customers are. Or they figure out how to do it faster or cheaper or better. Sam Walton's main innovation was to cut out the middleman, the distributor. This gave Wal-Mart the power to charge less than other stores, carefully manage inventories, and funnel the majority of its capital into expansion. Texan Michael Dell (Dell Computer Corp.) pioneered a direct sales model for personal computers in which he assembled the machines from generic parts and eliminated the retail layer. By effectively implementing this innovation, Dell has become the country's wealthiest computer hardware entrepreneur.

○ *Marketing*. The extreme entrepreneurs push the envelope peddling the stuff to the people. Mary Kay Ash, founder of Mary Kay Cosmetics, devised the original prototype for the infomercial: she trained her highly motivated salespeople to conduct two-hour "beauty shows" at the homes of willing customers. Going far beyond the Tupperware party concept, these demonstrations included personalized instructions on makeup and presentations on skin care.

EE Superstar: Steve Jobs

Steve Jobs is among the most extreme of entrepreneurs in history—and is in numerous ways the representative EE of our time. His iconoclastic, visionary credentials were established from the beginning, by proclaiming Apple's mission was to "change the world," and by acknowledging that his self-experiments with psychedelics and Eastern mysticism were fundamental to his inspiration. The story of Jobs' rise and fall at Apple is too well known to require recounting. What is interesting to highlight are his EE qualities, and these are evident from his post-Apple (and second Apple) phases.

> Steve Jobs is among the most extreme of entrepreneurs in history—and is in numerous Ways the representative EE of our time.

Jobs' phoenix-like is unique. Jobs has said that his creative models are Bob Dylan and Picasso—artists intent on continual re-creation of their selves and their work. This attribute—seeing your lifework as an art form—distinguishes the greatest EEs. As with most EEs, money is not a primary motivation for Jobs.

Soon after getting ousted from the company he co-founded, he rallied by forming NeXT computers. Not long after that, he bought into Pixar—a media animation company and thus a radical departure for Jobs, despite its high-tech basis. Though NeXT didn't fly market-wise, computer buffs were unanimous in their praise for NeXt's supremely fine hardware and software technology. The eventual purchase of NeXt Software by Apple for $400 million was a fitting culmination to the saga (although Apple spiked its plan to incorporate the NeXt operating system).

After a long buildup phase, the Pixar experience has proven to be a triumph for Jobs as well. Jobs' stature and salesmanship were responsible for the great terms Disney granted Pixar in their deal. And with both *Toy Story* and *A Bug's Life* hitting big at the box office and with the critics, Jobs has nothing but glory from this affiliation. Because Jobs can't contribute much to the technical side of Pixar's operation, his role there has been more relaxed one than at Apple.

Now Jobs has done the seemingly undoable: resuscitating a moribund Apple and restoring much of its former glory, and even profitability, during his second incarnation as Apple Headman. Perhaps the company will continue to rally—and at this point, no one should dismiss even shockingly triumphant possibilities—or maybe it will revert to its earlier decline. But no one can discount Jobs' achievement in rolling out the marvelous iMac and iBook machines. In many ways, these computers are a more perfect realization of the Apple spirit than even the Apple II and the Mac were in their time.

The greatest EEs possess the ability to grow, to preserve their vision by allowing it to evolve and never stagnate. In Jobs' case, his charisma and intensity seem to be undiminished, but his managerial self-control clearly has improved. Apple was his first love—a freewheeling, renegade company built in his own image. But his ultimate concern has always been the product, to make it "insanely great" and to market it with fitting style. After Jobs was stripped of his role at Apple, *Newsweek* asked him if he felt his company had been taken from him.

"To me, Apple exists in the spirit of the people that work there.

"So if Apple just becomes a place where computers are a commodity item and where the romance is gone and where people forget that computers are the most incredible invention that man ever invented, then I'll feel I have lost Apple.

"But if I'm a million miles away and all those people still feel those things and they're still working to make the next great personal computer, then I will feel that my genes are still there."

○ *Retail.* Extreme entrepreneurs reinvent the way stuff gets sold. Michael Cullen, who termed himself "the world's most daring price-wrecker," is considered the founding father of the modern supermarket. When he opened his Jamaica, New York, store in August 1930, Cullen was the first to merge a number of existing sales concepts: self-service, cash-and-carry, available parking, mass displays of groceries in clear aisles, the juxtaposition of low-markup and high-profit items, and newspaper advertising to spread the word. His groundbreaking concept was an immense success, and other food chains quickly adopted it, with A&P eventually becoming its leading proponent.

What's Stoking the Entrepreneurial Blaze?

With more than a million new businesses now started every year, how can we account for this record-breaking level of entrepreneurial activity?

Rulebreakers and Trendbuckers

Although the factors described below all seem to contribute to the current entrepreneurial climate, your own entrepreneurial motivation can hardly be reduced to one set of influences. One thing does seem clear, though: extreme or not, this is a great time to go for your entrepreneurial dreams. More people than ever in the history of inventing and selling stuff are going down the entrepreneurial road. Odds are, the more entrepreneurs out there playing the game, the more extreme entrepreneurs are out there breaking the rules.

○ *Debunking of corporate career path.* Not that EEs need any convincing, but entrepreneurship has never looked like such an attractive alternative to the rat race. Many people still see great value in working for a Fortune 500, but few "believe" in them anymore. Just as no one thinks that the large companies will be loyal to its workers, workers have no reason to be loyal to the corporations. The figures are revealing: in the early 1970s, one in five Americans worked for a Fortune 500 company; by the 1990s, the proportion had dropped to 1 in 10. The share of GNP accounted for by Fortune 500 concerns has been steadily dropping from the 58 percent high it hit in 1979.

○ *The American spirit—and a prolonged economic boom.* This is one potent combination. Deep down, that "Ben Franklin factor" is chugging away somewhere in all of us. In these auspicious times, it would nearly be a shame—downright unpatriotic—not to make the most of it.

○ *The Net.* Nobody *really* knows how long the online boom will extend, or how far down in our lives its impact will reach. And it's not clear yet whether the Internet represents a golden door of endless opportunity, a very exciting but dangerous Pandora's Box, or some wild combination of both. But it's here, enabling and spawning more growth and new businesses than ever before in the history of American business. A decade ago only a handful of people knew what the Internet was; now it's an industry and represents a huge new segment of the economy. Extreme entrepreneurs have been critical figures in this technological boom, and you'll bump into many of these heroes in the pages of this book. But even non-technological EEs are

Tangled Up in the Net

It's hard to nail down a perspective about the online dimension, for this obvious reason: this space is unfurling and shifting at hyperspeed. I don't want to dwell disproportionately on "Netrepreneurs," but the din of attention being lavished on these players makes it hard to avoid a premature Web-centrism. Due to relative novelty of the medium, the marketplace delirium, and media breathlessness, every new Net-commerce-concept entrepreneur can seem like a potential EE. Only time will allow the gold rush and musical chairs phase to subside in order to sort out the real EEs from the "Net-rich-quick" flashes.

Still, there are undeniable digital EEs. Jeff Bezos, for example, certainly qualifies. Even if his Amazon.com were to disappear tomorrow, Bezos' achievement has been so stunning as to place him squarely in the top ranks of entrepreneurship. He deserves credit for both vision and execution.

One of the hallmarks of an extreme entrepreneur is the ability to detect and leverage patterns, trends, and possibilities where no one's looking, and then seize the first-mover advantage before anyone even knows there's a move to be made. Bezos' primary "innovation" was simply in realizing ahead of others that the Net would be boundless. In May 1994, he read that Net usage was growing 2,300 percent a year. That's all it took...that, and the energy and brains to marshal the financial, logistical, and human resources needed to actualize his particular insight.

> **Only time will allow the gold rush and musical chairs phase to subside in order to sort out the real EEs from the "Net-rich-quick" flashes.**

Bezos' innovations include a fine-tuned inventory-minimizing logistics model, which expertly leverages information—as well as a network of strategic partnerships—to replace on-hand goods. In setting this up, Bezos took full advantage of the Web's strengths.

Another key factor has been the creation of a virtual community on the Web site. By featuring reader feedback, Amazon.com quickly became a human zone rather than just a commercial center. Before long, user "reviewers" began to engage through each other's critiques, producing a cross between letters to the editor and the Jerry Springer Show—something new under the sun. Though the idea of online community was already WELL-established (that is, starting with the Whole Earth

Net, continued

'Lectronic Link), Bezos successfully commercialized this quality—and numerous other sites are trying to follow its lead.

Bezos is a classic EE: fanatically intense, self-assured, and imbued with a "bring it on!" attitude about risk. Instead of resting easy with Amazon's pre-eminent ranking for online book sales, Bezos forged ahead into music and videos—and unseated CDNow (which had previously enjoyed first-mover advantage in online music sales) for the number one spot. But his master plan, if it succeeds, will make those achievements seem piffling: he intends to become the biggest merchant on Earth. Period. In pre-Net days, moxie such as this would make General George Patton blush; but now, it's an EE gamble with the biggest potential payoff in commercial history, or a shot at become a living symbol of Biblical-scope hubris.

naturally drawn to the possibilities this medium allows. They may just be inventing the next widget, but they're also figuring out how to use the Internet to sell more of their widgets.

○ *Dwindling options*. During the 1980s, business-related majors accounted for about one quarter of all undergraduate degrees, and a half million MBAs were awarded. Take large numbers of business educated people, combine that with corporate downsizing and outsourcing, and entrepreneurship starts looking like the best path to ensure personal economic opportunity.

○ *Set-up costs*. Not only has the cost of entry declined, but the perception of those costs has fallen as well. Launching a professional operation—including a one-person business—has been greatly facilitated by the availability of modestly-priced technologies such as computers (including laptops, organizers, and excellent software to run on all platforms), sophisticated telephony, and office equipment (copiers, quality printers, fax machines, and so on). In addition, transaction costs and the price of real-time access have plunged. The result is a much lower start-up bar in the crucial technology category.

○ *Availability of knowledge*. The entrepreneurship boom has led to an upsurge of interest among students, teachers, academics, journalists, and the general population. This result in turn becomes a cause. As the knowledge base expands, it generates more entrepreneurial efforts. Also, there is a new breed of entrepreneur—"repeaters," who start a series of businesses rather than sticking with one for their whole working lifetime. These "professional entrepreneurs" increase the pool of knowledge and encourage others to see entrepreneurship as a career in addition to a calling.

○ *Social evolution*. Although we have a long way to go, our society has made vast progress in the past several decades. One telling indicator is that American women are now starting more businesses than men are. These operations tend to be smaller, yet they testify to the powerful entrepreneurial spirit among women. Also, increasing numbers of African-American and Hispanic entrepreneurs are emerging, particularly as the middle class among minority communities stretches and expands. Asian-Americans have become a potent business force in all echelons of the economy. Another important tributary is the immigrant population, a greater-than-average percentage of whom historically have pursued the entrepreneurial dream. Within the Silicon Valley milieu, for example, look at Vinod Khosla, who co-founded Sun Microsystems at 27 and is now a partner at premier venture capitalist firm Kleiner, Perkins, Caufield, & Byers. This expanded sense of opportunity for anyone who's game plays a vital role in the national consciousness.

> One telling indicator is that American women are now starting more businesses than men are.

○ *SBA*. The Small Business Administration with its many branches provides essential expertise and support for start-up entrepreneurs and others scrambling to hoist their operations higher. Governmental agencies and private foundations have gone a long way in creating an entrepreneur-friendly environment. You can complain about Uncle Sam all you want, but the big guy does dig new business.

○ *Hipness*. "Everybody's doing it" is hardly a trivial factor. Cool kids used to buy Strats and form bands; now they buy stocks and form limited partnerships.

○ *Meaning and freedom*. This is the "last but not least" category. More than most other paths, entrepreneurship offers the chance to accomplish something with great personal meaning. It also answers the powerful craving to have some control over our own life and time.

In all, it's a combination of personal characteristics (the wild-eyed drive, etc.) and enabling conditions (advanced technology, a booming economy, etc.) that sparks the development of the extreme entrepreneur. But you'll get a better idea of what makes an EE tick as we move ahead and look at the extreme entrepreneur's innovations across the disciplines of business.

INNOVATION
and
Inspiration

The message of this chapter is paramount to your interpretation and appreciation of this entire book. It is focused on one underlying theme that is the hallmark of every successful extreme entrepreneurial venture: the dream—and bringing that dream to fruition.

All entrepreneurs directly or indirectly put forth a *unique selling proposition*, which is their vision—their big idea. This is their dream, and the shimmering gold in "them thar hills." The unique selling proposition, or USP, is a classic term in sales and marketing that pinpoints and succinctly defines one's specific product, service, or process and spells out why customers and consumers should embrace this concept over any and all others available at that time.

The USP is, in reality, the mini-mission statement that convinces customers and consumers to buy into your dream. If you look around, you will find your world is filled to the brim with products, services, processes, and concepts that you now heavily rely on—that you take

chapter

for granted and that were but ideas and dreams in the minds of extreme entrepreneurs only a few years or decades ago.

Consider that this includes everything from television, cellphones, and personal computers to frozen TV dinners and microwave ovens. As each new concept came forth and became indispensable in our lives—from the automobile, to everyday air travel, to communication satellites hovering in outer space—we bought into the USP put forth by the visionary entrepreneur behind it.

Every entrepreneur determines and defines his or her USP before venturing into business. He or she first decides what they want to do, offer, or make—and then goes for it. For example, the "cozy Euro-style café/newsstand geared to upscale locals." Or "specialty school supplies for the visually impaired." Or the "doorman-in-a-box locker that accepts package deliveries in your absence."

> Every entrepreneur determines and defines their USP before venturing into business.

Interesting ideas, all of them. Each with clear enough vision and a well-defined market. All the entrepreneurs who wield to these USPs would need to go to market is some seed money, a good plan, and a lot of luck. But there are no points for effort. Just because they may succeed in bringing great ideas such as this to market, it doesn't mean anyone's going to give a damn that they did. (What's that saying about a tree falling in the woods?)

Extreme entrepreneurs' USPs embody the revolutionary vision they are proposing. "Overnight delivery, anywhere, guaranteed" (Fedex); or "free email" (Juno); or "biggest bookstore on earth" (Amazon.com). All these phrases exemplify a promise—and ultimately, an achievement.

The point is, to be *extreme*—to break through with something original and compelling in an original and compelling way—calls for a USP that, along with the turbo-charged efforts of the entrepreneur, creates and drives success. When you see one of these USPs—and you'll *know* one when you see one—you can be sure there's an extreme entrepreneur standing right behind it.

The Extreme Golden Rule

All throughout this book you will find examples of extreme visionaries whose dreams changed lives. They have done so throughout history, and will continue to do so well into the future. How? By subscribing to the Extreme Golden Rule, which is:

Rules are made to be broken.

Well, broken, stretched, or made up from scratch. Extreme entrepreneurs do this because they *have* to, because their vision compels them to do whatever they have to in order to realize that vision, and they're fearless about breaking the rules.

Now don't go out there thinking this means that to realize your extreme dream, you should proceed recklessly and without discipline. Rather, first understand that we live in a world of rules. Business is a world of rules—extremely rigid rules.

To successfully *break* the rules, you must first understand the them. It is at this juncture that the extreme and the average in business invariably choose different paths.

While both types of entrepreneur may invest equal time and effort in learning the rules and principles of accepted business practices, the extreme faction sees them as goals rather than guidelines—and plunges wildly into carving out a new and uncharted path and a means of getting there.

Thus, rather than solely focusing on applying accepted theory and rules—such as developing a reasonable selling proposition—the extreme entrepreneur focuses on developing and implementing the dream instead.

And, as you shall see—both in this chapter and others—success can be exciting, intriguing, unpredictable, and rewarding, especially, when conventional thinking and stringent rules go out the window. A little bit of luck helps too.

It's a Wonderful Life

As noted, all entrepreneurs put forth a unique selling proposition—their vision and idea of how things can be made or done better in some way. But extreme entrepreneurs are those who fashion real breakthroughs, not mere follow-ups, extensions, or mundane elaborations on existing processes or technologies. Granted, while those who open a gas station, shoe store, or donut shop are indeed taking entrepreneurial risks, theirs are not extreme gambits.

One gauge, by comparison, might be to weigh the "impact" of an entrepreneur's efforts should it be removed from the big picture—much like that of Jimmy Stewart's life in the classic movie, *It's a Wonderful Life*. In this tale, Stewart sees how vastly different life in his little town would be had he not been there.

Along these lines, consider Emile Berliner, who invented the microphone. Without his pivotal contribution at the turn of the 20th century, others who followed would not have (and could not have) brought us many extreme entrepreneurial developments that we now depend on and take for granted in our everyday lives.

This includes the telephone, radio, TV, motion picture, and the entire music industry—to name but a few. Thomas Edison, Alexander Graham Bell, and Messrs. Metro, Goldwyn, and Mayer all thank Emile Berliner for his key contribution that in turn made their dreams possible.

Conversely, the open or closing of another neighborhood gas station, shoe store, or donut shop rarely has such impact as that of Stewart's movie persona or Emile Berliner's microphone. This comparison helps to narrow the scope and focus—and to better define the *extreme* entrepreneur.

Evolutionary versus Revolutionary

As an example, those who conceive, craft, and introduce a *new* type of kitchen stove—whether gas, electric, or wood-burning—are certainly entrepreneurs because they have entered into selling an idea, a *new* idea. But they would not be considered extreme, as they are simply furthering an existing concept. Thus, it is but an *evolutionary* process that simply furthers the concept of cooking and heating over an open campfire (by the direct application of heat) that has existed since the day of prehistoric cave dwellers.

Then comes Dr. Percy Spencer and a *revolutionary* idea that changed all our lives. His concept? Using high-frequency electromagnetic energy waves to penetrate foods and liquids, causing molecules to vibrate and generate heat for cooking and heating from the inside out, rather than by the direct application of an exterior heat source. The result? Today's microwave oven. Its speed and obvious benefits were an immediate no-brainer unique selling proposition for appliance manufacturers.

In retrospect, we see that by steadfastly developing and implementing his scientific dream, Dr. Spencer in turn launched a solid USP no one could argue. However, had he focused solely on the golden rule of developing a USP first, the microwave oven phenomenon would most likely never have happened—or at least, not in the way it has leapt into our everyday lives.

So, in reality, an entrepreneur's degree of *extremism* is proportional to his or her idea's revolutionary—not evolutionary—quotient. The extremist concept—whether a product, service, or process—is like a startling and fortunate mutation. EEs create entire new industries, revolutionize existing ones, improve peoples' lives, drive technological innovation, and foster social and cultural transformation. They tend to be the ones who imagine products or services that don't yet exist—the most visionary kind of entrepreneurship. They have the gift of seeing how customer tastes and habits are changing, and thus can "squeeze the value chain" to accommodate or accelerate these shifts. And that's just for starters.

> EEs tend to be the ones who imagine products or services that don't yet exist—the most visionary kind of entrepreneurship.

Why Didn't I Think of That?

How often have you said that when confronted with an obviously simple, yet profoundly necessary, new idea or product? It all boils down to opening up your eyes and mind, and to being keenly aware that tomorrow's revolutionary concepts are everywhere around you—and often it may take a second or third pass to make things work out right.

Rather than attempting to lead you through your world by the hand, pointing out extreme innovation possibilities, I'll offer the insights of Napoleon Hill to serve as a lodestar.

In his time-honored, best-selling book, *Think and Grow Rich* (Fawcett Books), Hill uses a series of short stories to make profound statements and drive home memorable points on perseverance, technique, and becoming an extreme entrepreneur. One such tale is "Three Feet from Gold."

This little story details how two lawyers from Boston ventured west during the gold rush era, and exhausted their entire fortune mining for this precious metal.

After almost a year, tired and financially tapped out, they turned their unsuccessful land claim and mining equipment over to an old desert

EE Superstar: Clarence Birdseye

The most significant innovation of Clarence Birdseye, a natural-born inventor and extreme entrepreneur at heart, was a freeze-drying method that did not degrade food taste or texture.

> His "discovery" was nothing more than nature in action, but it took Birdseye's inventiveness and drive to transform a natural process into a manmade one.

His "discovery" was nothing more than nature in action, but it took Birdseye's inventiveness and drive to transform a natural process into a manmade one. With the basic mysterious impulses that drive the majority of true keen-eyed would-be EEs, Birdseye dropped out of Amherst College just before his senior year and embarked on a fur-trapping adventure in Labrador. He returned home $6,000 richer, married, fathered a son, and then relocated the family back to the Arctic Circle.

In Labrador, Birdseye noticed food he put in the shed during the winter tasted fine and fresh upon being cooked weeks or months later. On the contrary, commercially available frozen food in the states was universally reviled for its mushy textures and tastelessness. Birdseye realized that the difference was the speed of freezing.

When exposed to exceptionally low temperatures, all the food freezes at once, producing a better tasting product when thawed versus the standard industrial methods where lengthy times in freezing the food allowed the slow formation of ice crystals that ultimately wreck the flavor and texture. Clarence returned to the United States and proceeded to develop a commercial fast-freezing technology.

But Birdseye couldn't get his company off the ground, despite his enormous effort and persistence, and high-quality output. He figured out the problem. His innovation was premature. The only establishments equipped with freezers back in the 1920s were restaurants, which were Birdseye's only steady customer stream.

Here's where he decided his USP was more than just terrific-tasting frozen food; it was terrific tasting frozen food for convenient use in the home. Because most grocery stores, and virtually all residences, still relied on iceboxes to store food, he started to shop around for a giant company with resources to build the infrastructure required for the ultimate success of his product.

Eventually, he found a buyer and sold his valuable patents to Postum Company, which immediately changed its name to General Foods Corporation and named its line of frozen foods after Clarence, separating his surname into two words. The selling price was $25 million.

vagabond and his donkey and headed on to San Francisco to recover and rebuild their lives. The old man decided to use the equipment just a bit more before tearing it down and selling it for salvage. The result? Well, it's not too hard to get ahead of this story, and to know that after drilling only three more feet, the old desert rat hit the largest gold strike in California gold rush history.

Napoleon Hill's point? How do you *know* when you're three feet from gold? And when *is* it time to quit? Perhaps the extreme entrepreneur believes he or she is *always* three feet from gold, and that's what keeps him or her going.

The Electric Flowerpot

One such example is that of a teenager named Joshua L. Cowan, who in 1895 invented the *electric flowerpot*. After months and months of planning, engineering, and adjustments, young Master Cowan proudly unveiled his creation—a slender metal tube with a battery inside and a bulb at one end.

When the tube was stood upright and pushed into the soil of a flowerpot, the bulb illuminated the plant's leaves and floral beauty hovering above. At night, it presented a stunning array of horticultural flora and fauna previously lost to darkness and shadows.

After putting together a dozen or so for his mother's flowerpots, Joshua waited for the world to beat a path to his door to snap up his electric flowerpot. Soon, a supportive uncle, Conrad Hubert, took interest and offered young Joshua a modest sum to purchase the rights to his invention. Uncle Conrad then set up a small factory and built hundreds of the devices, but soon realized the market for electric flowerpots was pretty thin.

Wracking his brain for a way to unload his inventory, Uncle Conrad toyed both with the product and its name. If not used to illuminate plants, then what? It was a light you could flash anywhere, ready for use when needed. Ready. *Ever*eady. Flash stick. No, flash*light*.

Thus, through second effort, young Joshua's invention leapt into the Entrepreneurial Hall of Fame as the *Eveready Flashlight*—and today, nearly everyone owns at least one "electric flowerpot."

To answer your question: "Why didn't I think of that?"—there is only this answer: perhaps you could have. If only you had looked at the world around you with fresher, wider eyes. Others have, others do, others will. So could you.

Oh yes, Uncle Conrad's Electric Flowerpot cum Eveready Flashlight Company went on to become Union Carbide. And young Joshua L. Cowan? Undaunted, he redirected his focus to inventing toys for children. How did *his* second effort fare? Hint: his middle name was *Lionel*.

The You in USP

By this point, you get the idea that the classic USP is more the cart that is pulled along by your dream rather than the horsepower that makes things go, and in the extreme entrepreneurial world, EE's tend to assign their own meaning to these letters.

In Joshua L. Cowan and Conrad Hubert's world, they had no clue as to a likely unique selling proposition. In fact, for the *electric flowerpot*, it would have proved fruitless. But, experimentation and second effort launched a whole slew of new "U's"—such as: unexpected (new uses), unleashed (new directions), unplanned, uncharted (new areas), leading to unparalleled, **U**ltimate **S**uccess **P**otential.

> Extreme entrepreneurs make a difference—and they won't let up until they do.

The lesson here? Again, know the rules when you start out, and then do not hesitate to bend 'em, shape 'em, and break 'em—until they serve *you*, and your goals.

It is said that a miniature billboard sits on Ted Turner's desk—a tribute to his father's original business. Upon closer inspection, the sign reveals one of the keys to Turner's brash but successful self-styled rise to entrepreneurial stardom. It reads: *"Lead, follow, or get out of the way."*

Extreme entrepreneurs make a difference— and they won't let up until they do.

A Card that Reshuffled the Deck

In the stories that follow, simple awareness and common sense are key ingredients that consistently triggered quantum leaps of opportunity for those entrepreneurs who were constantly poised and (ever)ready to *"Lead...and follow only their dream."*

Insights to Extreme Innovation

Research sponsored by the U.S. Small Business Administration (SBA) has greatly added to a better understanding of small firms as innovators. Here are a few notable points:

- Small companies (defined by the SBA as those with fewer than 500 employees) employed 53 percent of today's workforce, accounted for 47 percent of all sales in the country, and created 76 percent of all new jobs in the decade of the 1990s.

- Small firms provide the most initial on-the-job training. They are most likely to employ younger and older workers, to reach out to former welfare recipients and to recruit women—many of whom prefer to or can only work on a part-time basis.

- Small businesses produce 55 percent of all new innovations. They produce twice as many product innovations *and* significant discoveries per employee as do large firms.

- Small firms obtain more patents per sales dollar and on the whole produce far greater numbers of important discoveries per capita than do larger firms.

- While small firms produce the lion's share of patents and discoveries, they conversely garner only 11 percent of federal government research and development (R&D) dollars versus the 26 percent that goes to large firms.

> ## Small businesses produce 55 percent of all new innovations.

- The average small enterprise with intellectual properties has 61 employees—of which 19 percent are engaged in R&D. By comparison, the average large company with intellectual properties has 12,879 employees—with only 3 percent engaged in R&D.

- To facilitate R&D, the SBA implemented a new Small Business Innovation Research (SBIR) program in 1983 that has to date given 41,000 small businesses $6.5 billion in R&D awards—and the program is now growing by $1 billion annually.

- Among the important small firm innovations of the 20th century are the airplane, audio tape recorder, double-knit fabric, fiber optics, artificial heart valves, optical scanners, pacemakers, personal computers, soft contact lenses, and the zipper.

Source: 1999 *Facts About Small Business Report*, U.S. Small Business Administration, Office of Advocacy, Washington, DC.

Innovation and Inspiration

> **The seed of a revolutionary idea (and ultimately a truly unique selling proposition) can take many forms.**

The seed of a *revolutionary* idea (and ultimately a truly unique selling proposition) can take many forms, even that of an irksome dining situation. For example, in 1950 when Frank McNamara went to pay for a business meal in New York City and found his wallet empty, he experienced some on-the-spot embarrassment.

The restaurant manager mercifully accepted McNamara's promise to return with the money, so he was spared dishwashing duty. But that small embarrassing and uncomfortable event was forever etched into McNamara's mind. It spurred him on to ultimately envision and bring to fruition a *charge* card that would allow people to pay for meals in a range of restaurants on a credit basis.

He proceeded to found Diner's Club, and of course things really took off from there. The entire charge-card phenomenon derives from this single "EE moment." McNamara's receptivity to a need for convenience, based on a brilliant flash of insight, was supported with willpower to act decisively upon it. This set him apart from many others who had similar thoughts in equivalent situations, and put him well ahead of all who raced in to follow his lead.

The result: How many of McNamara's bright ideas do you have in your wallet today?

Credit Cards Got Folks to Thinkin'

While a wallet full of plastic forever changed the way we pay for or finance purchases of all kinds, another form of payment revolution now looms on the horizon.

The credit card was a logical answer to numerous problems and a USP no one could argue with. Consumers no longer had to haul cash or a checkbook on every outing, and merchants were assured of prompt payment within 24 hours. But that profound leap forward was (amazingly) 50 years ago!

Today, the lightning speed and global scope of the Internet are the driving force behind many business innovations—and the search for a new form of electronic currency hovers at the forefront of all e-commerce. The problem: How best to handle the millions in cash transactions now taking place every day? And the multi-gazillions expected tomorrow?

While increased Internet activity has given credit cards a welcome burst of new usage, both consumers and merchants instinctively know there is a better way out there/in there somewhere...and many determined extreme entrepreneurs are on a quest to find it, and to lay claim to the resultant rewards.

While existing services, such as Western Union, frantically wave their arms to draw attention and to be considered for money transfers, new and fresher concepts are offering more complete and convenient solutions for Internet users.

Adding P2P E-Cash to Plasticash

It began with online banking, which garnered only a lukewarm reception within the cyber-community. But this was only the precursor to a second wave of innovation that has sprung from this seed and is now growing into a driving force that has caught the attention of personal computer users worldwide.

At the forefront of the digital cash revolution, are virtual cyber institutions like X.com, which on the surface look and function like most other online banks and Web-based financial services available today. But the extreme difference lies in the fast and convenient new "person-to-person" (P2P) e-money services emerging.

Here's how it works. Let's say you and I have lunch. I come up $10 short. You loan it to me and I vow to repay it promptly. Here, as you are not a merchant, credit cards are of no help and thus my options are (1) mail you a check, (2) track you down and fork over the cash, or (3) buy you lunch next time we meet.

Now there is a (4): *PayPal* (a service division on X.com), and a number of other similar person-to-person payment and e-currency services, whereby you and I deal directly and electronically. I just log on (in this example) to X.com's Web site, enter your e-mail address, indicate the amount of money to be sent (in this case, your $10) and the info on my credit card to which it is to be charged—and clicko *presto*—you've got $10 parked and waiting for you when you return from lunch and open your e-mail.

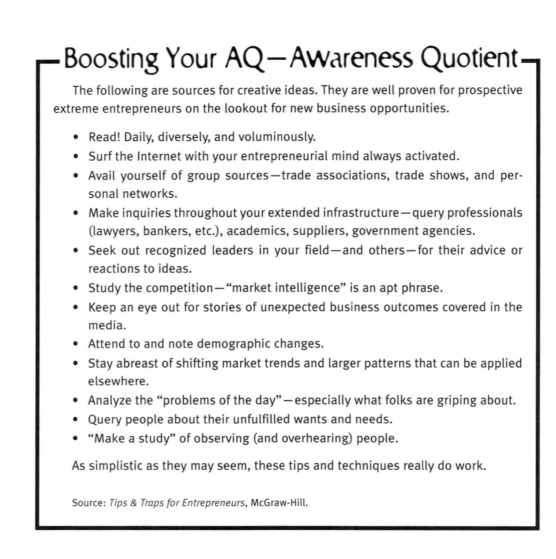

Boosting Your AQ—Awareness Quotient

The following are sources for creative ideas. They are well proven for prospective extreme entrepreneurs on the lookout for new business opportunities.

- Read! Daily, diversely, and voluminously.
- Surf the Internet with your entrepreneurial mind always activated.
- Avail yourself of group sources—trade associations, trade shows, and personal networks.
- Make inquiries throughout your extended infrastructure—query professionals (lawyers, bankers, etc.), academics, suppliers, government agencies.
- Seek out recognized leaders in your field—and others—for their advice or reactions to ideas.
- Study the competition—"market intelligence" is an apt phrase.
- Keep an eye out for stories of unexpected business outcomes covered in the media.
- Attend to and note demographic changes.
- Stay abreast of shifting market trends and larger patterns that can be applied elsewhere.
- Analyze the "problems of the day"—especially what folks are griping about.
- Query people about their unfulfilled wants and needs.
- "Make a study" of observing (and overhearing) people.

As simplistic as they may seem, these tips and techniques really do work.

Source: *Tips & Traps for Entrepreneurs*, McGraw-Hill.

Your options are: (1) tell the issuer to deposit it in your checking account (done so within 24 hours), (2) apply it as a credit to any credit card balance of your choice, (3) have the bank cut a regular check and send it to you via snail mail, or (4) withdraw it instantly from any ATM anywhere on earth. Whatta deal!

The best part, over and above the speed and convenience, is that it doesn't cost me *or* you anything. Nope, it's free (for now, at least). So how do online banks make money? Just like brick-and-mortar banks do, by offering free P2P e-cash transactions as a loss leader and counting on other chargeable financial services to generate income.

Handy and fast, P2P e-cash is already being used by millions world-wide, and—as more uses and applications are realized—this hot new innovation is expected to sweep the cyber world with warp speed application. Online auctions have already felt the surge, and many small office/home office (SOHO) companies are picking up on the obvious benefits. Parents now use it to send Johnny and Susie some occasional spending money at college. Office workers have discovered it as a great way to gather cash from colleagues for everything from birthday gifts to sports betting pools. And that's just the beginning.

What else? Your cell phone and palm pilot will open the door to a new world called: micropayment, whereby you will be able to dial in and e-pay for mini-purchases like newspapers from a street vendor or a soda from a vending machine.

The bandwagon is rolling, and everyone is hopping aboard. As more companies and institutions start offering P2P e-cash services (both free and with modest service fees attached), its growth is expected to be viral in nature. Everyone who receives such payment must only register to get their "free" money—and who wouldn't? The extreme entrepreneurs behind this power-fully attractive USP are today earning hundreds of millions of dollars over and over again for simply implementing their dream. Soon, it will be billions.

Beyond that, the vast potential of the cyber-universe lies waiting for anyone willing to explore that which seems virtually limitless. It is *still* a largely untapped vein of opportunity and wealth where anyone with vision and foresight is just "three feet from gold," and where incredibly wild success is truly within your grasp.

Need more encouragement? Think opportunity isn't everywhere? Think again.

The Good (to the Last Drop) Life

Howard Schultz is the extreme visionary who turned Starbuck's into today's mighty purveyor of the designer coffee experience. He did so by coming up with a multi-layered unique selling proposition that is an unmatched blend (coffee terminology, if you will) of product, marketing, *and* management.

When Schultz experienced Milan Italy's vibrant café and espresso culture, he realized there was a huge untapped market category to be mined back home in the United States.

And he was right. Once Americans had a taste of the real deal, most would never go back to the roadside diner's endless cup-o'-joe. Since caffeine is also somewhat addictive, we're talking about a truly captive audience for Schultz and Starbuck's, offering vast lifetime profit potential.

Thus, whatever was good "over there" is good here as well. (Why didn't *I* think of that? Schultz *did*—and reaped the rewards.) In subsequent chapters, we'll also take a closer look at the marketing and management techniques that propelled his empire to enviable heights.

Here's another tale where an extreme entrepreneur's steaming cup of great thinking and good fortune runneth over.

Tea — It's in the Bag

Not every successful innovation involves a new—or, at least, *totally* new—selling propositions. Here's a case where a brilliant flash of distinctive, functional product repackaging was pretty much the sum total of the USP—and to stunning effect.

Thomas J. Lipton was a masterful marketer, and became a millionaire before getting involved with the product that bears his name. Born to a poor Scottish family, Lipton had become an exceedingly successful grocery entrepreneur in America. He'd always intended to popularize Britain's favored beverage—tea—on our coffee-swilling shores, and a plan gradually took shape.

First, he blended his own tea, and by cutting out the middleperson reduced the price considerably. He also pre-packaged his tea in convenient sizes—quarter-pound, half-pound, and pound—which reduced the need for customers to have it measured out individually. He also came up with offering it to America's hot beverage drinkers in convenient individual dunk-and-brew tea bag increments.

With this simple, but completely fresh approach to his product and customer, he scored big. As an added bonus, his unique packaging concepts kept the leaves fresh, so the end product retained quality and had a longer shelf life.

Bottom line? Same stuff, extreme presentation.

Napster Judgments

So often, incredible success springs from new approaches to the most common and widely used things. In these few examples alone we've seen vast fortunes made by simply rethinking the approach and usage of everyday things—like transferring money and drinking caffeinated beverages, such as coffee and tea.

Next comes recorded music and Napster, and another wildly successful revolutionary idea based on a basically simple concept and dream. In the waning months of 1999, two college students—19-year old Shawn Fanning and 20-year old Sean Parker—got an idea and launched a little start-up company in San Mateo, California, offering free software that allowed home computer users to easily trade music files over the Internet. Within only a few months, it became the proverbial "shot heard 'round the world."

So often, incredible success springs from new approaches to the most common and widely used things.

In the early months of the year 2000, while Internet cyber-citizens (mostly college students) were feverishly swapping and duping their favorite music tracks, the recording industry took note and bolted into action to stop this blatant piracy in its infancy. But things are not always as simple and clear-cut as they may at first seem.

Without delving into the inner-workings of the dispute, there are perhaps solid arguments on both sides pro and con—but more important, it has sparked a controversy that extends far beyond just Napster, Napster-like companies, and the entire worldwide recording industry. Today, Fanning and Parker's little idea represents a whole new way of exchanging information and, regardless of how the legalities of exchanging music files eventually plays out, the basic concept is now out there. The genie is out of the bottle, the toothpaste is out of the tube, and there is no putting it back.

In reality, Napster's concept is painfully simple: instead of storing *anything*—whether millions of songs or the bios of the lovelorn in search of each other—Web sites now just become listing directories and portals enabling person A to contact person B for just about anything, only directly. Newer variations on this theme even cut out the Web site middleperson by offering free or licensed software that links computer users *directly* with each other (such as Gnutella), answering informational requests without passing through an intermediary, who may charge a fee for delivering the goods or passing the inquirer on to another destination.

Just like when Marc Andreesen and a handful of students at the University of Illinois created and introduced their revolutionary software application called Mosaic—the browser tool that gave life to the World Wide Web concept—thanks to Napster, the universe of the Internet will never be the same again.

Like monetary micro-payments and P2P e-cash transfers, this peer-to-peer file sharing is yet another looming concept destined to prove that from tiny acorns (of ideas and dreams) the mighty oak (of prosperity and success) does grow.

By pursuing a dream, two small extreme entrepreneurs have unleashed a force destined to impact the lives of almost everyone on this planet in one way or another.

Shake, Wrap It, and Roll

Owners of a small drive-up barbecue joint in San Bernardino, California, Richard and Maurice McDonald foresaw the huge demographic shifts that were about to take place at the close of World War II.

As the boys came home from "over there," the McDonalds saw substantial numbers of the population starting to relocate from cities to an outer landscape being quickly forged beyond the city limits. In addition to noticing this suburbanizing of America, the McDonalds were also aware that a large percentage of women who'd joined the workforce during the war were now opting to *stay* employed. As a result, many working mothers had little time for or interest in the elaborate food preparation of days gone by.

Based on these insights, the McDonalds created a new type of food purveyor to answer the need, and the fast-food restaurant, as we know it today, was born. By 1948, they'd invented and implemented all the basic components: precision food preparation, fast and tightly guaged cooking times, constant cleaning schedules, full mechanization, and price appeal.

They even understood the value of expanding through franchising; by 1954, they'd sold 21 franchises. Ray Kroc was merely a milkshake machine salesman who was fascinated by what the McDonalds had wrought.

When *Grinding It Out* (St. Martin's), a biography of Kroc, was published in the late 1970s, the McDonald brothers were furious. In the book, Kroc dates the company's birth to 1955, when he opened *his* first franchise. This was later revealed to be a complete crock of Kroc. Though it's incontestable he was the force behind McDonald's growth into the world's predominant burger monger, in reality Kroc hadn't actually *invented* or *created* anything.

In the 1998 *New York Times* obituary for Richard McDonald, he was quoted in 1991 telling *The Wall Street Journal*, "Up until the time we sold, there was no mention of Kroc being the founder. If we'd heard about it back then, he woulda been back selling milkshake machines."

The result? Kroc knew a good thing when he saw it, and he did not hesitate to act on it, even if it involved climbing on the back of someone else's idea and concepts. Had he carved out his own USP? Probably not. But sometimes teaming up with others who have unearthed extreme potential can be a good thing, and arguably better than struggling to do so on your own.

> Sometimes teaming up with others who have unearthed extreme potential can be a good thing, and arguably better than struggling to do so on your own.

So Where Are Bill, Martha, and Post-It™ Notes?

Within these pages you will certainly encounter many hugely successful individuals whose innovations have become an on-going part of our everyday lives. But I'll also point to some lesser known and emerging extreme entrepreneurs, exciting and unique new concepts, and a wealth of clever ideas and resources intended to stimulate your thinking and nudge you out of the role of passive observer.

What has transpired business-wise throughout history, and up to and including today, is just that—*history*.

Drucker: The Sources of Innovation

The hands-down winner as greatest business thinker of the century, Peter Drucker, is a master at synthesizing huge amounts of information and extracting core principles. In his summation of entrepreneurial innovation, there are seven fundamental sources from which breakthroughs spring.

1. *The unexpected.* The "unexpected success" is sometimes a form of sheer serendipity, but often it's an indication that further innovation is required. When a company finds a "tail that wags the dog," chances are that management strategists are holding the dog backward. Unexpected failures also demand rethinking. Unexpected outside events often contain kernels of opportunity. All these "unexpecteds" make demands on entrepreneurs to apply intelligence.

> **Unexpected outside events often contain kernels of opportunity.**

2. *Incongruities.* These are only apparent to those already in a particular industry. They can take many forms: incongruities between economic reality and expectations, between perceived and actual customer expectations, between reality and assumptions about it, etc. Incongruities mean there's an error or a gap to discover or fill.

3. *Process need.* This refers to some concrete need, not just to opportunity. An innovation based on such a need must satisfy five criteria: it must be a self-contained process; only one weak or missing link; a clearly defined objective; clear specifications for a solution; and high receptivity. Further, there are three key constraints: you must truly understand the need, not merely sense it; the knowledge to solve it must exist already; and the solution must fit in with the actual way people work.

4. *Industry and market structures.* Industries can change through rapid growth, convergences of hitherto distinct technologies, or modifications in how business is done. Insiders usually respond to such seismic shifts as a threat, but for outsiders opportunities abound.

5. *Demographics.* Population shifts occur continually, and resulting patterns create and negate business opportunities. The population changes may relate to education level, class, ethnicity, gender, or age.

6. *Changes in perception.* Many developments can qualify here: Emerging ideologies, fads, spirit of the times, cultural preferences. Timing is essential to catch these waves.

Innovation, continued

7. *New knowledge.* This category garners most of the hoopla when we think of innovation, and it does offer very special returns and possibilities. But it also entails special risk. Frequently the result of converging knowledge or technologies, these breakthroughs require entrepreneurs to quickly focus on the strategic opportunity, and to establish themselves as market leaders. On the downside, shakeouts begin as soon as the window closes, and most players do not survive. Plus, markets aren't always receptive to new knowledge-fueled innovations. This class of development is highly unpredictable.

Source: *Innovation and Entrepreneurship*, Harper & Row.

Starting with your dream and the desire to make a difference, you will be challenged to delve deeper into the mechanics and rationale that can help set you and your endeavor apart from the pack—not simply by choice, but by performance.

Opportunity today is unfolding at warp speed, as evidenced by the Internet and e-commerce. Just a few short years ago, embryo companies like Yahoo! and Amazon.com were but wild concepts illuminating a new frontier. Now, they are the contemporary success stories everyone seeks to emulate.

> Opportunity today is unfolding at warp speed.

Today, wild new concepts are reshaping old arenas—and they will perhaps be outdated and old hat by the time you read this. But at this moment, lavish big dollar game shows and reality TV—like *Who Wants to Be a Millionaire?* and *Survivor*—and mammoth best-seller books, like the Harry Potter series, are the Camelot *du jour* of two staunch and heretofore highly established industries. They all help prove that nothing is immune to a powerful idea whose time has come.

By now you understand that high-profile extreme entrepreneurs—both historic and contemporary—may achieve celebrity, but their unique selling position, brilliantly executed, is just the start of it. Their USP is only good and secure until someone like you comes along and challenges their position.

Within these pages my interest lies in helping you structure a challenge to any and all existing positions. Today's new opportunity and your burning desire to make it happen make it easy to envision you being tomorrow's extreme entrepreneur success story—and in this chapter, we've done so without *once* mentioning Bill Gates and Martha Stewart as a stellar learning experience (at least for now). And that's a good thing.

II

part

EXTREME BEGINNINGS

On the path from pure inspiration to actual inception, entrepreneurs must make a series of tough and strategic nuts-and-bolts decisions they hope will help them to live long and prosper.

This includes a punch-list of everything—from the pros and cons of partnerships and the art of naming a company for today's new breed of consumers to deciding where to situate operations and deciding whether it needs to be a "bricks and mortar" physical business or a broad-based, non-tangible, Internet-only "cyber-shop"—or both. (Phew!)

For a start-up neophyte, grappling with such complex and high-stake choices is like being at a crossroads without a map. The high percentage of first-year business casualties attests to the numerous perils and pitfalls of the start-up phase.

Even among seasoned entrepreneurs and the extreme faction within this group, plenty have wiped out early in their first, second, or third attempts, proving that even those with great business destinies aren't always immune to early, fundamental blunders.

Thus, success begins with a deep awareness that without an effective structure to support it, even the most innovative business idea is merely potential energy.

The more *extreme* the venture, the more important clear definition, precise planning, and razor sharp focus becomes.

START-UP
Finessing the
Particulars

This chapter zeros in on some of the serious issues at stake in an entrepreneurial start-up. While there are many fundamental decisions that greatly influence the dynamics of any burgeoning company, key elements that tend to have a particularly decisive impact include:

- Partnering. Combination dynamics. Is it better to fly solo or with co-pilots?

- Name game. Naming a business or product in today's cluttered environment.

- Technology. Strategic application of emerging technology creates opportunity.

- Business plan. Is it just a piece of paper or does it really play a role?

- Location. Considerations on where. Bricks-and-mortar or on-the-air/cyber-shop?

chapter

The other major component is, of course, capitalization. Money, cash flow, and the generation of dinero are such major factors in business start-up and the on-going process of doing business that capitalization certainly deserves and ultimately demands its own chapter. So stay tuned for Chapter Five, *Gassing Up the Tank*.

Meanwhile, look for a moment at these variables from a garden variety, off-the-rack entrepreneur's perspective for a quick-drying process business.

Partnering. Should I go into the emergency location cleaning business with my brother-in-law or should I get a loan and go it alone?

Name game. Should I call my emergency drying process Dry-Tech, Qwik-Dry, or NoH_2O?

Technology. Should I spend time and money developing an online component to my new business or stick with our traditional business model until I've established a beachhead?

Business plan. How do I write a plan that will convince the bank I've got a shot with this thing?

Location. Should I take that cheap warehouse space three towns away until I get profitable?

These are good questions, and just the tiniest fraction of the endless number of such start-up questions a would-be entrepreneur should be asking of his or herself. But what do these same sorts of questions look like in the go-for-broke extreme entrepreneur's thought balloon?

Partnering. Should I hook up with my former archrival in a strategic alliance that brings ready cash to my venture to the tune of multi- maybe mega-millions of dollars?

Name game: Should I call my company WorldDomination.com or CrushtheCompetition.com?

Technology. How can I best use every level of advanced technology at my disposal to permeate every conscious aspect of my market's existence?

Business plan. These brilliant ideas scribbled on both sides of a paper napkin ought to do the trick, eh? (Or will it?)

Location. Should I be where the smart, hip, motivated workforce of the future is? Or stay in my mother's garage until I make my first billion?

I'm only somewhat kidding here. Even the most basic of start-up consideration is always on a far grander scale for the entrepreneur whose vision is so big and compelling that it threatens to swallow whole everything in its path. For the *extreme* entrepreneur, that is.

To We or Not to We?

Partnering decisions—whether to and, if so, with whom–carry extremely high stakes. Such choices not only can determine a company's ultimate success or failure but, just as important, have an enormous impact on the quality of an entrepreneur's experience.

> Partnering decisions carry extremely high stakes.

Pitch-perfect partnerships are hard to beat. History (both distant and recent) is rife with business get-togethers that conjure up images of mega-success within given arenas. In the world of building aircraft, Messrs. McDonnell and Douglas took Wilbur and Orville's idea to new heights. In household product pioneering and manufacturing, things got far better for all of us when Mr. Proctor was introduced to Mr. Gamble. In personal care products, Messrs. Cheeseborough and Pond reigned supreme with slick ideas from cold cream to Vaseline®. In retailing, pairings like Neiman-Marcus, Sears-Roebuck, Hammacher-Schlemmer, and Lord & Taylor are legendary.

The financial world and stock market greatly profited from the teaming of two young newspaper reporters—Charles Dow and Edward Jones—in 1882, which fostered both the oft-quoted Dow-Jones averages and the esteemed *Wall Street Journal*. Later, investors got another boost when Messrs. Merrill and Lynch teamed up with their original partners Pierce, Fenner, and Smith.

In the world of sawdust entertainment, one great partnership—that of Phineas T. Barnum and J. A. Bailey—brought showmanship to new heights. A later double-deal with the five Ringling Brothers made their combined three-ring circus the undisputed "Greatest Show on Earth."

On the other hand, hostile partner dynamics and relations can make life unbearably tense and unpleasant. Most disastrous *failures* (due to improper match-ups) are logically less well known, because they were…well, disastrous from day one. They of course precluded the likelihood of days two, three, and so on.

EE Superstar: Trammell Crow

"Partner" is one of Trammell Crow's favorite words. During his ascendance to becoming "America's biggest landlord," as *The Wall Street Journal* dubbed him, the charismatic, Dallas-based real estate tycoon spawned a dense network of partners across the country (though concentrated in several hubs, with Dallas the principal one).

Crow was an exceptionally creative extreme entrepreneur in a raft of ways, and he took huge delight in the interpersonal aspects of doing business. Apparently, he took the greatest pleasure in dubbing new "partners," particularly when the fortunate honoree wasn't even expecting it. Crow would find a deal that attracted his interest, and choose as a co-partner some young man whom he liked — "someone you like to see coming into the room," he once said. He wanted partners with drive, discipline, brains, and a good spirit. Naturally, the deal would be consummated with nothing more official than a handshake.

> Crow was an exceptionally creative extreme entrepreneur in a raft of ways, and he took huge delight in the interpersonal aspects of doing business.

Crow then would bankroll the project, hand off as much responsibility as the new partner could handle, and go 50/50 on the returns. Crow would help out with advice and know-how, but the level of trust he offered astonished the neophyte partners, who, naturally, supplied the sweat equity.

So this is how Trammell Crow established his empire — not through despotism (absolute authority), but munificence (liberal generosity). It hardly needs saying that all these bright, competitive, and usually wealthy men were fanatically loyal to their Texas Santa. With his hugely lucrative cult of personality, Trammell really had something to, well, crow about. He believed in sharing the largesse, in the human satisfactions of forging a brotherhood, and also in the business advantage of having strong people behind and around him. It provided great leverage.

Eventually, many years after his beginnings, he saw to it that his haphazard league of "franchisee" partners was organized into a coherent business that would outlive him. He entrusted the mission to his unofficial business heir, J. McDonald Williams, a man whose demeanor was completely different from Crow's. Williams was phenomenally smart and a natural leader due to his many abilities rather than the effect of charm. Crow had no doubt the younger man deserved credit for turning Trammell Crow Company into a great organization. While Williams imposed structural and procedural discipline that rendered the operation "coherent," as he put it, the Trammell spirit carried on as long as the founder was around. Today, the company continues to prosper while Trammell Crow himself has recently retired.

Despite the absence of a sexual dimension (in most cases), the relationship between entrepreneurial partners is frequently as intense and consuming as that of a marriage. Business partnership has also driven a wedge between siblings in countless situations. Blood may be thicker than water, but often it is not as thick as the "company ink." For these, and loads of other reasons, business partner *counseling* (an important new subset of mediation) is a thriving field.

By their very nature, many extreme entrepreneurs are constitutionally unsuited to the give-and-take a partnership entails. Their intensity, determination, self-assurance, and autonomy are antagonistic to cooperative decision making. The more self-aware among such entrepreneurs recognize their propensities and limitations at the outset, and thus opt to go it alone. Conversely, those who go against their instincts usually find themselves in unworkable situations, where one partner winds up having to buy or force the other out.

> By their very nature, many extreme entrepreneurs are constitutionally unsuited to the give-and-take a partnership entails.

But a sizeable percentage of EE partnerships have also proven to be powerful and durable unions. The theme that generally predominates in such stories of successful teaming is one of *compatible competencies.*

That is, both parties bring different—but essential—ingredients to the mix, and their divergent aptitudes don't work at cross-purposes; rather, they harmonize. Each partner has his or her own, somewhat separate role. Yet the combination also produces a synergy—whereby they absorb and learn from each other's perspective, and thus the collaborative decision-making process produces far better solutions than either would or could come up with on their own.

Yin and Yang of Partnering

One common partnership dichotomy is the *thinker* and the *doer.* This combo is also known as the *visionary* and the *technician.* Such a blend is especially potent during a company's early years, when the business is running at a high entrepreneurial pitch. It's crucial to have a visionary—the inspirational leader, the galvanizer, the spark. But it's just as critical to have someone anchoring a rapidly rising business with their outstanding ability to get the job done.

A good example of this is the teaming of Richard W. Sears and Alvah C. Roebuck on April 1, 1887. Prior to this date, while working for the railroad, Sears discovered the salability of ornate pocket watches—quite by accident—when a local jeweler refused a shipment of time pieces. Purchasing the lot at bargain basement prices, he began selling them to his fellow time-conscious railroad employees at a handsome profit.

Encouraged by the response, he ordered more and repeated his success over and over until he decided to establish the R.W. Sears Watch Company in Minneapolis, Minnesota. Needing a competent watchmaker on staff for repairs, Sears ran a want ad and Alvah Roebuck responded. The rest—as they say—is mail-order history.

The interesting partner footnote? Obviously there is no Roebuck in Sears today. Why? In short, Sears was the thinker, the visionary—and Roebuck was the doer, the fixer who rounded out the picture. As the company grew over subsequent years, the thinker and visionary's role expanded, while the doer's role evaporated into multiple roles many others could play as well or better. I'll take a closer look at some innovative Sears thinking a little later on.

Often, the visionary can profit immensely by having a doer-partner to help implement the conceptual dream. In the end, they will generally grow apart as the visionary continues to explore new ideas and concepts while the doer perfects and performs the day-to-day tasks previously launched.

Auto Biography Insights

Another key combination to note is the *visionary* and the *manager*. This salt-and-pepper blend of personality and functionality is a necessary duality for sustaining a creative company over the long haul. In such a setup, day-to-day leadership may either be shared or fall entirely under the manager's purview to keep the dream intact and operational.

From the outset, Henry Ford's vision of building automobiles by assembly line was only possible to sustain through decade-after-decade of process and product evolution with a logical two-tier application of both the manager and doer concepts.

Lucille Ball and Desi Arnaz
Til Debt Do Us Part

Married partners form a business category totally unto themselves. If the relationship is a stormy one, obviously that can introduce another layer of managerial "noise" and interference to deal with. But when a marriage is smooth running, such a partnership confers advantages: the two executives know how to discuss, compromise, and collaborate.

Of course, if the marriage hits the skids, the business arrangement is more than likely to spin out as well.

The most fascinating aspect here is the partnership dynamics between the principals. The extreme entrepreneurial union between Lucille Ball and Desi Arnaz is a front-runner in this regard. Married in 1940, both were enormously talented entertainers—Ball as a comic genius, and Arnaz as a musician and showman. As an example, one night in Cuba, he spontaneously invented the conga line. While he and Lucy both had strong entrepreneurial mentalities, Arnaz, in particular, was an amazingly shrewd and visionary businessman.

> **Married partners form a business category totally unto themselves.**

After forming Desilu Productions in 1950, Arnaz cleverly finagled ownership of the early *I Love Lucy* episodes from CBS. He deployed this cache by pioneering the concept of reruns, allowing him to establish a highly profitable TV empire. In fact, Arnaz was a maestro of extreme innovation—as the first to (1) save a show on film, (2) use three cameras, and (3) perform a sitcom before a live audience.

In 1957, fleet-footed EE Desi Arnaz worked out a deal to buy RKO film studios from CBS for a modest but undisclosed price. The next year he turned around and sold the 180 early Lucy episodes back to CBS for $4.3 million.

However, from its inception the Desi/Lucy partnership was strained. The very existence of *I Love Lucy* was predicated on salvaging the marriage, as it would require them to work and spend time together. But Desi's compulsive drinking, reckless gambling, and—above all—blatant womanizing was ultimately unacceptable to Lucy.

When they finally divorced in 1960, Desi Arnaz received an undisclosed cash settlement. After their split-up, they still tried running Desilu Studios as a team, but that proved untenable. Lucy, the stronger manager of the two, bought out Desi in 1962

Ball and Arnaz, continued

and in 1967, sold off the debt-ridden Desilu Studios to Gulf & Western, for a cool $17 million.

The two (once dynamic EE partners) did, however, remain close friends until Desi's death in 1986 and he remained in Lucy's warm words and thoughts up to her death in 1989. The stormy Desi/Lucy partnership was not unlike the volatility found in many close-knit business ventures where founders or principle players are also married; theirs was just high profile and more visible than most. It was also a good lesson in common pitfalls.

At either level, Ford was always the visionary and the font of fresh, creative energy—the spark plug. *Managers* then kept the engine revved and production wheels turning by keeping the workforce fired up, operational, and working smoothly. In turn, thousands of *doer*s were first driven and propelled by the explosive force of the visionary and then consistently maintained and kept running by the steady hand of a capable manager.

There are, however, many good examples of successful yin and yang combinations and true partnering within the evolutionary history of the automobile, and on a much different level than Ford's. One is the unlikely and extreme blending of Charles Rolls and Henry Royce.

In 1904, Rolls was a high-profile, "mud and guts" derring-do race car driver. Known as an automotive maverick, he was a self-promoting showboater, a clever auto innovator—and a true visionary. In other quarters, a quiet and concise young Royce manufactured varied mechanical products and slowly built his business on a reputation of quality and lasting design.

When they met (quite by chance, through a friend) Rolls, carefree daring vigor proved to be the ideal match for Royce's thorough and intricate mechanical thinking. To the table, one brought flare, style, and showmanship, while the other brought obsessive attention to detail. Together, these qualitities became the Rolls-Royce hallmark neither could have, or would have, ever achieved on their own.

In such a partnership, the maverick is often channeled and reined in by the more stable of the two. The result is a faster, more exciting ride for the plodder, and a greater likelihood of extended viability for the shoot-from-the-hip visionary.

When Two Heads Are Better Than One

In a similar partner teaming, another duo demonstrated how a single design modification turned the automotive industry on its ear. In 1900, Austrian engineer Emil Jellinek helped Germany's famed Daimler Engine Works develop a revolutionary automobile—with the engine situated in *front*, rather than behind or under the driver— which they then named after Emil's daughter, Mercedes, as a tribute to his design breakthrough.

This incredible modification in car design sparked industry-wide change, but it wasn't until Daimler merged with another German firm in 1926 that the company was propelled to the highest echelons of world-wide automotive industry and history.

This partnership with the notoriously conservative Karl Benz, who had initially resisted this profound paradigm shift, formed the company today known as Mercedes-Benz.

Much like Henry Royce, Benz was renowned for high-quality engineering and overall excellence. This is where the unique selling proposition took its critical turn: through partnership, the Mercedes was first and foremost revolutionary and then went on from "just" an automotive innovation to being an innovative product rooted in excellence, the Mercedes-Benz USP that stands to this day.

The moral is Daimler's Mercedes innovation only pushed into extreme territory when it was dovetailed with Benz's reputation for engineering and quality.

These basic *visionary* and *technician* and/or *manager* distinctions aren't absolute of course, and some EE teams shift from one role to another. Often one or the other will have a slight edge in a given capacity, and so they'll agree, explicitly or tacitly, to assign that dimension to the partner with more flair for it.

For a good example of this shifting combination, we'll delve into the Apple Computer story, which is discussed in detail later in this chapter. The tumultuous partnership between Steven Jobs and Stephen Wozniak continually vacillated and both rebalanced and redefined the importance of their respective roles as company visionary (Jobs) and hands-on manager/technician (Wozniak).

Also, as you will see in the case of the two Yahoo! founders, people who might not necessarily be hyper-ambitious on their own *can* (and often do) add up to far more than the sum of their parts in tandem and through teamwork.

Some of the benefits of partnership are intangible. Even the most extreme of energetic and highly motivated entrepreneurs can experience lags in enthusiasm or fortitude at times, and the moral support inherent in a tag team can help prevent energy crises.

Finally, *companionship* shouldn't be discounted as a desirable motivation factor in commerce as well as personal life. After all, "It's lonely at the top," and it's lonely at the outset—and, often, it's lonely in between.

> Some of the benefits of partnership are intangible.

Two Shiny Red Apples

The Apple Computer saga offers an interesting two-parter: first, a visionary/technician-doer combination that worked fine, followed by a disastrous shot at a visionary/manager alliance.

The two Steves—Jobs and Wozniak—formed a textbook example of the messianic promoter joining forces with a gifted technical whiz. Once Apple was off and flying, tech Wozniak apparently believed his work was finished, so he moved on to other things, namely finishing up the college studies he abandoned to build Apple with the visionary Jobs. Meanwhile, left unchecked, the unpleasant underside of Jobs' mercurial personality began to undermine the company.

Jobs expected everyone to share his missionary overdrive in quest of "insanely great" technology and market triumphs. He found it difficult, if not impossible, to conceive that Apple's employee force didn't all crave 80-hour workweeks. Further, it didn't occur to Jobs that he might ruffle egos when he summarily dismissed others' ideas as worthless whenever they didn't jibe with his own views. Without Wozniak to ground him and provide a reasonable balance to his passion, Jobs was running on fumes and soon everyone (including Jobs) knew it.

Just a Couple of Yahoo!s

One high-tech partnership apparently made in heaven.com is the one that begat Yahoo!—Dave Filo and Jerry Yang. Both are very smart, but

Caution, Danger Ahead

A slew of events may trigger the dissolution of business partnerships. Among the most common are the following:

- *Managerial disagreement*. A rift occurs in the their strategic visions.
- *Fade-out*. One partner relinquishes their portion of the job.
- *Divorce*. When a partner divorces a spouse, the business partnership is often next.
- *Spouse onboard*. One of the partners wants their mate (often a new one) on the top management team.
- *Catastrophe*. One partner gets hit with an unforeseeable event disabling them from maintaining a role.
- *Sex*. One of the partners develops a hankerin' for the other, complicating or stressing the relationship.
- *Shift in market position*. It's just as stressful when a company's fortunes suddenly soar as when they suddenly plummet.
- *Business cheating*. One or the other partner violates their business agreement, for example by branching out in a side venture that draws customers away from the company.
- *Money*. A partner wants to take more capital out of the business than the other partner is willing to part with.

Dave is the brilliant one, technically. Of the two, Dave's the more reserved thinker, whereas gregarious, Taiwan-born Jerry was the first to snag the vision of an hierarchical Net directory—inspired, he says, primarily by Dave's preternatural ability to *find things* online.

The two have divergent personal styles, but compatibility requires more than merely attraction of opposites. In a 1997 interview, Dave had only this to say about his business mate: "Jerry's cool." Jerry, on the other hand, had plenty to say about Dave. "We probably couldn't have found two better partners [than] each other in the business sense. We're both extremely tolerant of each other, but extremely critical of everything else. We're both extremely stubborn, but very unstubborn when it comes to just understanding where we need to go....We've both been through some rough times [but] we've never had rough times together....It's just a fantastic relationship, and I hope it's a lifelong one." As do Nasdaq investors.

The Yahoo! story unfurled like a buddy movie. Once the two became Web fanatics, they started compiling a list of favorite sites. Then they categorized their list, and subdivided it, and sub-subbed it. Soon, they started getting outside hits, sparked by word-of-mouth and e-of-mail. They were spurred on by sheer momentum, competition (from search engines such as Lycos and a couple of other directories, such as the World Wide Web Virtual Library), and joyful camaraderie. Jerry said it was "...like driving off a cliff. Like *Thelma and Louise.*"

> The Yahoo! story unfurled like a buddy movie.

Yahoo!'s explosive trajectory and market dominance are now history, and most agree that it was Yang and Filo's partnership that made Yahoo!'s genesis a most excellent adventure. Without that bonding and mutual encouragement, neither one of these EEs seemed likely to make it happen alone.

A Pair of Walkmen

One of the powerhouse business partnerships of modern times was between Sony founders Masaru Ibuka and Akio Morita—both EEs to the core. Ibuka's original vision was to use transistor technology to make radios portable and strong enough to make civilization accessible to everyone in the world. Although Ibuka didn't himself invent transistors, he was the first to see their potential in such a transcendental framework—and to surmise how profitable such a plan might prove to be.

Ibuka and Morita met during World War II, and soon afterwards set up shop together in a bomb-ravaged Tokyo department store building. Ibuka was the technician—albeit one with an especially elevated perspective and ambition—while Morita was a master in sales and finance. Within these extremely different but complementary roles, both men found they upheld precisely the *same* business philosophy: success arises from doing what others are not.

In its effort to exploit semiconductor technology, Sony became the world leader in miniaturization—which was a precondition and the precursor for producing the small transistor radios that were Ibuka's original vision.

For the full span of their careers, Ibuka and Morita held fast to their maverick pledge, developing one after another generation of fantastic technology products and masterfully building new markets for each. Among their bellwether creations were the transistor TV (1960), the Betamax VCR (1975), and the Walkman (1979).

Throughout rapid growth and global expansion, the partners easily maintained their respective roles. Ibuka devoted himself to product development—the body and soul of Sony's sales proposition—while Morita designed and executed the innovative marketing concepts and techniques to carve out new niches in unexplored territory that were, by comparison, the proverbial heart and mind.

Johnson & Johnson (& Johnson!)

Just as extreme entrepreneurial partners with the right chemistry often yield extraordinary results, the combination of incompatible ingredients can just as readily catalyze disastrous chain reactions. As mentioned earlier, those who share the same blood chemistry can make for especially volatile agents.

When the three Johnson brothers, Robert, James, and Edward Mead (who preferred to use his middle name) consolidated their entrepreneurial energies to form Johnson & Johnson in 1885, they forged a formidably balanced triumvirate. Robert, the eldest, was a dominating sort ideally suited to serve as president and chief administrator; James was the dedicated engineer; and Mead the outgoing chief salesman.

As their surgical goods company prospered nicely, however, the partnership increasingly foundered. Robert's absolutism and Mead's headstrong ways clashed continually and vehemently, until it drove Mead to branch out on his own. Robert had long opposed Mead's desire to manufacture pharmaceuticals, so Mead finally found the perfect opportunity to pursue his own vision. Thus, he created Mead Johnson & Company, which ultimately became a pioneer in the baby food industry. Fortunately, once the brothers severed their business cords, amicable family and company relations resumed.

It is also interesting to note that in 1920, the technically-oriented James Johnson— least flamboyant and most reserved of the three brothers—was responsible for introducing the one single product that made Johnson & Johnson a household word. His tinkering led to what quickly became one of the most famous trademarks in the world: the *Band-Aid*.

Tune that Name

To extreme entrepreneurs, branding is no casual pursuit. They understand the horsepower of a product, service, or company concept more often than not hinges on a distinct name that boosts recognition, memorability, and ultimately—marketability.

Undeniably, some monikers lodge in the mind better than others, or have more of a twang. One name often rolled out as a supreme example of form fitting function is Jiffy Lube—a tag that concisely describes what they're selling.

The reasoning behind, and connection between, a product and an inspired name can also create resonant and lasting mental associations. For example, Steve Jobs claims to have named Apple to commemorate a happy period he spent working on a farm. As for being a revolutionary "knowledge tool," Jobs'Apple echoed everything from the Garden of Eden beginnings to the gravity of Isaac Newton's discovery.

> To extreme entrepreneurs, branding is no casual pursuit

Sometimes, extreme entrepreneurs look close to home for naming inspiration. In 1951, Chicago bakery owner Charles Lubin set out to mass-produce exceptionally high-quality cakes. He named the business after his own teenaged daughter, Sara Lee. When Ruth and Eliot Handler invented a new, revolutionary type of doll for girls in 1958 (Barbie), they named it after their daughter, Barbara. When the doll became a huge worldwide super-seller, the Handlers decided to give Barbie a male companion (Ken). Following suit, they named it in honor of their son, Kenneth.

Many entrepreneurs find the simplest name for a product or company is their own. For those with the right ring to their name, this is the ultimate solution. For example, did Max Factor have to look any further?

The ABCs of Choosing Identity

Initials and the occasional acronym offer another approach. The full, worded name defines the company with precision, but sometimes the abbreviated form gives it wings.

Trademarks — Law and Order

Once you've come up with a name for your company, it's time to protect it. Why? By law, it is an "intellectual property" — an asset created by the mind — and you own the rights to your creation, just as an author owns the rights to a book, a composer a song, or an inventor a better mousetrap.

It is real property that can be sold, rented, or licensed to others — and it becomes more valuable with use. It never wears out, and every dollar spent promoting it increases its worth. With care, your rights in a strong trademark are absolute and eternal. Thus, it is worth protecting — and knowing how to do so.

Officially known as *The Trademark Act of 1946*, and universally known as, "The Lanham Act," U.S. trademark law is remarkably simple and sensible, and here's everything you need to know:

- A *trademark* is a proprietary name that identifies something. It doesn't have to say this is a "good product," just that it is "the same type and quality" of product as you've purchased previously. It can be a word, a design, or a combination of both.

> **With care, your rights in a strong trademark are absolute and eternal.**

- *You own a trademark* in the United States simply by using it. Your rights are established by active commercial use, not by registration — which is only legal documentation of ownership and an official record that you use a particular trademark.

- *You register a trademark* by informing the U.S. Patent & Trademark Office that you're using it, and what you're using it for. If they indicate no one else is using it for the same (or a confusingly similar) class of goods — and if nobody objects after they publish it in the weekly *Trademark Official Gazette* — it's yours. In 1988, laws were revised allowing applications to be filed before a trademark's actual use in commerce, and the reservation of a trademark for six months to three years before actual use.

- *Registration lasts* as long as you actively use a trademark, but you must file an affidavit of actual use in the sixth year of registration, and then renew it every ten years. The purpose of these laws is to prevent as few words as possible being removed from our language; when you stop using one it's automatically returned to the common lexicon.

Trademarks, continued

- *You cannot register* generic words (or obscene material). While the law forbids registering "apple" as a name for fruit—or even "pomme," which is French for apple—you can register "Apple" as a name for something else, like a computer.
- *The law says*: "If your new trademark may cause a significant minority of the audience to confuse your products with those of another company already using an existing, similar mark (registered or not), you can't use it."

That's the whole foundation of U.S. trademark law, and what you need to know to protect your company identity.

Courtesy of NameLab, Inc.

Some acronyms will always work better than others. That's why most company founders ponder such matters long and hard to achieve just the right phonetic flow.

For starters, familiarity and simplicity are always a strong duo—and ABC is about as good and basic as it gets. DEC is also a good example of a double duty letter/word combination (a successful and easy-to-remember acronym resulting from the computer giant's first attempt to be known as Digital Equipment Corporation). However, the AOL trio still remains one of the most memorable and pleasing trio of letters ever assembled: tuneful—much like an upscale French name.

In general, though, the downside of initialized names —such as IBM— is their sterility and facelessness. IBM was later unofficially warmed and humanized by the corporation itself with the nickname "Big Blue." Radio and TV stations, which are designated only by call letters and numbered frequencies or positions on the dial, have always had to deal with this dilemma, and their general solution has in turn been to coin and promote a strong tagline. As an example, Chicago's superstation—WGN, owned by the Tribune Corporation—stands for the *"World's Greatest Newspaper."*

Making Names an Art Form

In the early 1980s, about the time the business world suddenly became energized, choosing a name itself became a business. Big business. Soon, along with the advent and spectacular growth of the Internet, dot.coms, and youthful techno-moguls, there was a new dependency on word science and the needed expertise of niche companies like NameLab of San Francisco.

For two decades now, this company of highly educated linguists has quietly teamed up with major corporations to create new words they believe you and I will quickly come to know and love. And based on their successes to date, they are most often right on target.

These namesmiths first carefully weigh the message to be conveyed. They then run the message, point-by-point, through the company's proprietary bank of assembled morphemes of the English language— which are simply isolated semantic elements (like the "van" in Advantage)—that express any aspect of each desired message they input.

These morphemes are then combined in various ways and endless combinations to construct or create new or existing words or catchphrases that convey as many aspects of the original desired message as possible. The result? Some of NameLab's familiar creations include: Acura, Compaq, CompUSA, Geo (automobiles), Lumina, Luxor, The Olive Garden, Slice (soda), and Zapmail.

In recounting how the Acura name came about, NameLab president and founder, Ira Bachrach, notes, "Honda had a line of very well respected cars (named after company founder Soichiro Honda), but wanted to also build and introduce a high-end line to rival the luxury automobiles of Europe. Honda had established itself at a particular level in the mind of the consumer, and to gain ready acceptance of increased pricing for their new upscale product, the company needed a new name with an immediate connotation of a highly engineered vehicle along the lines of Germany's Mercedes-Benz."

So into the hopper went the elements of Honda's desired message and out came NameLab's dream sheet of desirable morphemes that said it all. "The competitor's hallmark was obviously engineering and visions of skilled technicians in white lab coats feverishly making notes on clipboards supported with key imagery and buzz words like mathematics, metallurgy, and precision. We took these words apart in every way imaginable. The result was to focus on accuracy...accura...*Acura*, and it was the first Japanese car that Americans acknowledged and embraced as being a true prestige automobile."

A Titanic Launch

Picking a name or slogan that will be used internationally can be a tricky business. Many brands, trademarks, and catchphrases haven't always fared so well. Here are a few classics and well-circulated industry bombs to demonstrate ill-researched (and ultimately disastrous) product names or catchy slogan roll-outs that sank numerous agencies and companies alike.

- When General Motors introduced the popular Chevy Nova in Central and South America, who knew that "No va" in Spanish means "it doesn't go!" Yikes!
- The Dairy Association's popular slogan "Got Milk?" bombed in Mexico when it came to light the literal Spanish translation read: "Are you lactating?" Sales quickly dried up.
- Coors beer anxiously launched its slogan "turn it loose" in the Hispanic market only to find that once translated into Spanish it happily foretold that you will "suffer from diarrhea." Oops.
- When a Scandinavian vacuum cleaner manufacturer first brought its product to America, they proudly proclaimed: "Nothing sucks like an Electrolux." Hmmmm....
- Clairol introduced its new "Mist Stick" curling iron in Germany before first learning that "mist" was slang for manure in that country. Few Germans had use for the new and exciting "manure stick."
- When Gerber began selling baby food in Africa, they were miffed at poor sales, until they learned that in Africa, many people can't read, so companies always put a picture of what's inside on the label. Thus, Gerber's smiling baby wasn't a big seller.
- Colgate marketed a new toothpaste called "Cue" in France—only to find it was the name of that country's number one porno magazine.
- An enterprising T-shirt maker from Miami hastily made up Spanish language shirt's for the Pope's visit—with one minor flaw. Instead of saying: "I saw El Papa (the Pope)," they read, "I saw la papa (the potato)." Pope, potato, pototo...
- The ad agency guys at Pepsi were shocked to find its "Come alive with the Pepsi generation" slogan for the Chinese market was literally translated as, "Pepsi brings your ancestors back from the grave." Some bought with great expectations.

> **Picking a name or slogan that will be used internationally can be a tricky business.**

Launch, continued

- Coca-Cola in China (depending on regional dialect) also translated into either "bite a wax tadpole" or "female horse stuffed with wax." Savvy Coke execs quickly changed the corporate moniker to read "Kokou Kole," meaning "happiness in your mouth."
- Chicken king Frank Perdue's poultry slogan, "It takes a strong man to make a tender chicken" was a disaster in Spanish, translating out as "it takes an aroused man to make a chicken affectionate."
- Parker Pen took it's ballpoint pen to Mexico with the proud slogan, "It won't leak in your pocket and embarrass you." Instead, the second to the last word somehow became "embarazar," thus assuring it would not "impregnate" you. The population was relieved.
- When American Airlines advertised new leather seats for first-class flights to and from Mexico with it's "Fly in Leather" slogan, they were shocked to find it translated literally into Spanish as "Vuela en cuero"—"Fly Naked." Indeed!

The moral of these stories? Choose (and translate) your words carefully!

The Picks of a Picker

When asked what he thinks are some of the best names around, NameLab's Bachrach offers up Dave Filo and Jerry Yang's "Yahoo!" without hesitation. Why? It is Bachrach's contention that a highly descriptive, inspirational, or engaging name is a powerful secret weapon that unquestionably gives one company a competitive edge over others.

Bachrach has said that Yahoo! is perhaps the greatest brand name of the last 20 years because, "At the time, they weren't the only search engine around, yet they took the mundane process of finding the information you were looking for and made it sound like fun. It led you to believe it worked, and that you would exclaim 'Yahoo!' as a result. Was their technology any better? Who knows.

"Their name certainly was, and it worked. Had they called it InfoBank...WeFind4U... or lotsastuff.com...things probably would have turned out quite differently."

Another favorite is Spam, the name chosen for George Hormel's ham-like product made of chopped pork. As it wasn't directly from the pig's hindquarters (which legally defines "ham"), the FDA nixed Hormel's referring to it as canned ham. In an effort to rename his new pork loaf, Hormel decided to introduce it to party guests at his home as an *hors d'oeuvre* with a proviso that—with each drink ordered—a guest must offer up a new name for the mystery meat. Requesting his fourth martini of the evening, with a cube of whatever poised atop his toothpick, an unemployed radio actor named Kenneth Daigneau blurted out "spam" to the bartender. The drink arrived, the *hors d'oeuvre* disappeared, and SPAM was born.

Other Bachrach favorites include those names that became synonymous with an entire genre of product. Examples include: Xerox, Kleenex, Jell-O, Aspirin, Formica, and Jacuzzi—to name but a few—all of which began purely as product names.

Why Two Ks

George Eastman said the word *Kodak* was the result of a highly deliberative process. He "knew a trade name must be short, vigorous, incapable of being misspelled to an extent that will destroy its identity and, in order to satisfy trademark laws, it must mean nothing." He'd always thought highly of the letter "K," which was a fashionable naming letter of that era—and he decided to start and end the word with it. So he tried on thousands of phonic variants, and Kodak was the result. After his camera was a huge success, this extreme entrepreneur wisely renamed his business *Eastman Kodak*—which was a huge improvement over his then Eastman Dry Plate Company.

> A trade name must be short, vigorous, incapable of being misspelled to an extent that will destroy its identity and, in order to satisfy trademark laws, it must mean nothing.

Seventy years later, Eastman's verbal acuity had a direct influence on Chester Carlson's name choice. His company, Haloid Corporation, was located in the same town as Kodak, Rochester, New York, where Eastman was a legendary figure. So when Carlson sought a catchy name for an innovative photocopying machine, he decided to repeat the first letter to end the word (in the Kodak/Radar vein).

He'd already decided to base the product's name on a Greek root word meaning "dry," and with his Kodak-inspired addition he came up with Xerox. Once Haloid's technology caught hold, Carlson changed the company name as well.

About this same time, in the era of popularity for Ks and Xs, the names for Kimberly-Clark's Kleenex tissue and Kotex products were also chosen based on the same select letter rationale.

Naming in a Hyper-Cyber Business World

Bachrach's NameLab itself is a perfect example of the hyperspeed in which today's business world is unfolding. While on one hand his company is a model of contemporary thinking, he is setting it up to be devoured by other Bachrach extreme innovations now being introduced on the Internet.

These include a number of edgy *InstantIdentity*.com Web sites enabling one to inquire, select, and easily buy a business identity online (at a fraction of the cost) versus doing so via his existing "brick and mortar" physical shop in San Francisco.

"I realized we're probably eating ourselves in the process," notes Bachrach, "but hey, if we don't—some other young and eager upstart company will. Better we evolve quickly and remain a key player in the name game."

Here Bachrach touches on one of the key truths in the fast-paced world of extreme business maneuvers. One can no longer afford to start with one good idea and then simply keep collecting data and experience along the way. All it does is weigh you down and make you vulnerable to new, fleet-footed competitors.

In today's hyper-cyber business world extreme entrepreneurs must view all new services, ideas, and ventures as *fuel*—rather than items to collect—which they pull in, compress, and use to propel them on to the *next* opportunity, much like a jet engine.

> In today's hyper-cyber business world extreme entrepreneurs must view all new services, ideas, and ventures as fuel

That is precisely what Bachrach is doing with his existing "bricks and mortar" NameLab and his new Internet *InstantIdentity*.com cyber-shop. It's Bachrach's "jet fuel."

"I Got One Word for You, Kid…'Internet'"

In the classic movie the *Graduate*, Dustin Hoffman is whispered one single word intended to impact and shape his future destiny. That word? "*Plastics*." In the late '40s and '50s, that was probably pretty good and sage advice. Plastics were the new and hot emerging technology of the day…then.

Today, that *word* could very well be computers, Internet, intranet, bio-genetics, or any one of a number of emerging new technologies shaping the year 2001 and beyond.

The majority of extreme entrepreneurs naturally find emerging technologies downright irresistible, especially when these technologies can confer competitive advantage. Though conventional wisdom cautions against early adoption of new, often bug-laden technology, EEs generally aren't inclined to bide their time until the all clear is sounded.

Historically, the success of some EE start-ups has been at least partly attributable to the coincident emergence of new technology. The reason Henry J. Heinz' second venture flew so well after his first one crashed and burned may owe much to the development of the pressure cooker and automatic can-making in the interim.

Henry Ford's use of assembly lines is an even more obvious example. Although it was actually Ransom E. Olds who pioneered the mechanization of car-making when he opened the country's first car factory in 1899, and applied a rudimentary form of the assembly-line method.

A more recent, well-known example of an extreme entrepreneur who leveraged a still-young technology is Ted Turner, whose media achievements can be traced back to his early use of satellite transmission for his first, small TV station.

Then, of course, there are companies such as Dell Computers, which couldn't exist were it not for numerous high-powered technological advances and widespread deployment. Michael Dell has made brilliant use of the Internet (which allowed him to dispense with middlepeople in his business concept), and also developed top-flight assembly plants and streamlined distribution channels.

Turn On, Plug In, Roll Out

There's been a cascade of recent breakthrough technologies that upgrade business efficiency and improve the chances of success for smart and compact extreme entrepreneurs. As computer, software, Internet, and telephony capabilities progress at near warp speed, prices are falling at a near-equivalent pace.

For the first time ever, tiny companies of only three or four people can emulate much larger operations with sophisticated communications technologies that allow them to access and utilize market research data, implement low-cost production, and respond to market demand.

What hardware doesn't accommodate, reasonably priced service companies do. For example, businesses that send faxes only infrequently can dispense with a machine by using one of the many new online fax services. Want to back up and store vital computer data? No need to buy costly software programs and high-capacity disk drives when you can do so inexpensively (or for free) at specialty Web sites on the Internet. And so on....

Some of today's most potent technologies for cutting edge extreme entrepreneurs are:

> ## What hardware doesn't accommodate, reasonably priced service companies do.

- Bar code systems. These have facilitated widespread adoption of Just In Time (JIT) production and distribution—a technique that was deployed as far back as the early days of Ford Motors, though in a rudimentary form.
- Powerful new software such as Enterprise Resource Planning (ERP), which integrates all departments and functions across a company into a single computer system. Doing so allows different departments to share information and communicate with each other. Some other examples are Contact Management programs and Computer-Assisted Design/Computer-Assisted Drafting (CAD) and Computer-Assisted Manufacturing (CAM).
- Wireless communications. Within facilities, between locations, or with suppliers.
- Broadband transmission, which is a type of multiple data transmission in which a single medium (wire) can carry several channels and signals at once. Cable TV, for example, uses broadband transmission.
- The Net(s)—Intranets and Extranets as well as the Internet.
- Web sites that offer free, or nearly so, services to entrepreneurial start-ups; for example, Bigstep.com offers free e-commerce-enabling services that help create or manage a Web site, market your business online, sell products with secure e-commerce, implement e-newsletters, etc.
- Faster, more powerful, and extremely portable electronics.

In the largest sense, Dell's overarching achievement is in implementing one-to-one direct marketing on a mass scale in a big ticket, high-dollar market. (Hewlett Packard actually *followed* Dell's lead in this.) Similarly, Amazon.com has leveraged advantages across several major technology brackets—relying on the integration of communications and logistics systems, and redefining bookselling as we know it in the process.

When it comes to deploying technology, IBM's much-heralded one word slogan of years gone by still warrants a spot on your bulletin board: *Think*.

"Got Another Word for You, Kid..."

If plastics were the key to the '50s and Internet savvy the gateway to the '90s, then *Intranet* strategy is fast becoming the success buzzword du jour for EEs of the new millennium. "Say what?" you ask.

Not all extreme entrepreneurial successes are necessarily *new* ventures into the world of business. Rather, one unique twist today is that many start-ups—looking to find or establish a niche in cyber-based e-commerce—are taking a page from some long-established corporate behemoths who have found a way to totally revitalize rather than going the way of many other "brick and mortar" big business dinosaurs. And vice versa.

Consider Weyerhauser Company, a major player in the manufacture of custom residential and commercial wood doors. Windows and doors are the number one dollar volume product category in both new construction and remodeling, and until a few years ago the company's 12 to 15 percent market share was impressive.

But as both time and technology marched on, the now 100-year-old timber company's techniques—both for manufacturing and sales—came under pressure. With the introduction of hi-tech communications, from fax to e-mail, for everything from ordering to assembly and distribution, the old way of doing business now slowed the process, bloated costs, blew sales, and brought morale to an all time low. Weyerhauser was under pressure, sales figures were slipping and something had to be done.

Like many companies—both high- and low-tech—Weyerhauser first turned to the Internet and created a Web site with all the basic *normal* bells and whistles: types of products offered, about our company, and how to contact us, etc. Yet, it only represented a faster and slicker way to do the same old thing. Customers and salespeople still had to laboriously wade through the painstaking job of planning and ordering custom-built doors

Social Climbing versus Business Climbing

In 1992, entrepreneur and mountaineer Ann Krcik launched *Extreme Connection*, a promotional agency for outdoor athletes. Despite the extreme nature of her actual business, she soon found herself pinned at home by a whirlpool of administrative tasks and growing correspondence.

Now new technologies have come to the rescue, restoring some of her freedom and permitting her to travel for business more frequently. Today, she brings her PowerBook laptop computer everywhere, even on multi-day rock climbs, so she can send and retrieve e-mails; a wireless modem attached to her cell phone makes her accessible even when bivouacked 4,000 feet up on a sheer cliff face.

Today, extreme success not only lies in employing new technologies in your business offering, but in your execution as well. Keep up with all that's new—and use it to your advantage to gain an individualized competitive edge.

literally from *two million* different configurations and options—from size, style, and color to surface veneers, core options, and hardware. Then, should one decide upon a little round window for some pizzazz, local building codes might require that it also have triple-glazed tempered glass with a one-hour fire-resistant core to offset the potential hazard of this nifty little opening—or, maybe not. Researching local codes alone often took weeks.

Making matters even worse, once an intricate door configuration *was* decided upon, the cumbersome custom assembly process was set into motion. How? A handwritten sheet was taped to a core material, which was then sent off down the line to be sized, drilled, milled, covered, and stained—just for starters. The problem? These sheets often fell off and were found on the floor. Where two lay, a guessing game ensued—and often, cross orders resulted when the sheets were transposed. Without going too deeply into all of the company's problems, let us shift to the turnaround and the amazing solution.

The Intranet and E-Engineering

In 1995, Weyerhauser began phasing in a new technology called *Intranet*, whereby their existing Web site was totally overhauled, revamped, and expanded into a tool for fool-proof and rapid *e-engineering*. In essence, it became a small internet universe of its own within the vast global Internet.

Start-Up: Finessing the Particulars

71

Today, customers and distributors alike go online and tap into Weyerhauser's powerful *DoorBuilder* program. There, they wade through the company's millions of door options in a matter of minutes and easily sidestep time-consuming errors in a nanosecond.

Want brass hinges on your door with three screw holes in each? And you live in Tuscaloosa, Alabama? Oops! Local code requires this type of door to use *titanium* hinges with *four* screw holes per hardware unit. (However, if you lived in Minneapolis, it would be okay.) The system spots this instantly, offers the correct solution (saving perhaps a week's delay), and moves on to the next category.

When the order is complete, a simple click on "submit" unleashes a sophisticated updated manufacturing and tracking process that has brought the company into the 21st century, increased market share from 12 to 26 percent, and dramatically increased bottom line profits. The program has been a gleaming example of better productivity through technology.

Beyond simplifying the process and increasing efficiency, the *DoorBuilder* program has unearthed volumes of invaluable info revealing everything from inventory overstocks and discrepancies to situations whereby some dealers, once thought to be valuable assets, were (in reality) deadweight losers costing far more than they were actually bringing in. The benefits were vast and key to Weyerhauser's establishing a niche in Web-based e-commerce.

Through the extensive and expansive *DoorBuilder* Intranet e-engineering program, Weyerhauser has attained much more than mere survival. Whether you are an extreme high-concept start-up, or an existing high-tech/low-tech business feeling the crunch, new and emerging technology can and will start you off with a competitive edge and/or keep you abreast of the pressures of aging.

For more information on this valuable emerging technology, visit *Intranet Design Magazine's* portal site on the Internet at <http://idm.internet.com> or check out *Intranet* on various search engines like Google, Jeeves, and Yahoo! It's worth the effort if you want to become or remain a frontrunner.

Visit to the Promised Plan

There are many reasons to complete a comprehensive business plan. Historically, the unspoken imperative to compose a business plan has been a "given."

Simply put, for both everyday entrepreneurs as well as extreme visionaries, probably the three best reasons are:

1. It causes you to thoroughly focus on your idea from start to finish and to get a better grasp on the realities of your concept. In doing so, you'll be surprised how many potential pitfalls appear that are more easily dealt with in the planning stage—rather than after you've allocated resources ineffectively.

2. It becomes the best way to communicate your ideas to others—whether to solicit potential customers, potential partners, or investors. No bank, private party, or venture capital firm will lend an ear, let alone a chunk of capital, to any entrepreneur who lacks such a comprehensive, organized document. Of course, the plan must strike potential investors as plausible and reflect favorable financials for them to consider risking their money. However, red flags in all sizes and shapes can shoot up if an entrepreneur's plan is deficient or flawed in any of the following ways:

   - Due diligence about the market and the competition is skimpy.
   - Time or revenue projections seem excessively optimistic.
   - Important factors are missing or vague.
   - Logic is sloppy.
   - Projected scenario lacks flexibility or includes no alternative tactics.
   - Unfilled slots or weak spots in the management team.

   Assuming the entrepreneur passes the business plan hurdle, with some luck the team will be granted an audience with the solicited investor. The in-person meeting is of the utmost importance; in most cases, this is the deciding factor for the final yes/no verdict. Investors want to see a confident, coherent, convincing presentation to kick it off, but they're most interested in the team's intangibles, its spirit.

   A sound business plan should be revisited frequently as a refresher and reminder of your original concept and goals.

3. A sound business plan should be revisited frequently as a refresher and reminder of your original concept and goals. Without doing so, it is easy for problems to escalate in tiny increments to such a point that your current operation is far afield of your original intent. Many companies make an annual review part of their standard operating procedure to be sure

they remain clearly on track. This ensures they don't fall behind the curve, merely running on autopilot, or miss opportunities to cut costs or innovate.

But at this point, a powerful business plan becomes an even more instrumental tool for the extreme entrepreneur, as they are often dealing with less tangible concepts—and certainly, are proposing a fresh new approach to whatever they set out at.

In the hands of a skilled EE, a stellar business plan—one carefully crafted to answer questions and build a vision in the mind of a potential partner, investor, or lender—is an invaluable asset and an ally of epic proportions. Properly structured, with just the right balance of blue sky possibilities and down-to-earth realities, it can garner believers and set hearts to beating faster—just like your own.

In the early days of your dream, your plan is perhaps the best ally you can have. Besides yourself, it is certainly the best salesperson. Thus, it is imperative that you build your first partner—your business plan, the blueprint for your dream, the roadmap of your vision—with care. With extreme care.

Know/Show Business Plans

Sitting on the highest rung of Silicon Valley VC firms, Draper Fisher Jurvetson is considered some of the *smartest* money in the world. Timothy Draper told a reporter that they receive roughly 10,000 business plans a year, hold initial meetings with only 500, and ultimately finance about 15 on average.

"What DFJ partners are looking for," he says, "are the most obsessive, visionary, inspired entrepreneurs. Those whose business plan reflects clear goals that outline a drive and desire to remake, redefine, or dominate some aspect of their chosen world."

On another occasion, Jervetson said he would sometimes give the nod to "an average idea backed by a fantastic entrepreneurial team," but would never fund even the world's most unique idea "if they consider the team behind to be less than stellar." Obviously, a cozy family restaurant, conceived by Steven Speilberg and George Lucas, would fare better with Draper Fisher Jurvetson than a far-reaching, state-of-the-art virtual reality theme park conceived by your mom and her bridge club.

Still, a strong and engaging business plan is the single best wedge you'll have to pry the entry hatch ajar (and, not infrequently, some well-placed connections will help too). While would-be customers, possible investors, and potential partners want to see a glimmer of true passion and commitment in the entrepreneurs they interview in person, a well wrought paper business plan mustn't contain any eager panting or overzealous testifying.

As evidenced by the extreme entrepreneur's ability to successfully get up and running, they obviously—in some way and each in their own distinct style—mastered the necessary nature of a successful business plan or prospectus. In varying ways, they managed to present a statement of condition—unembellished, free of optimism, frank, and conservative—that demonstrated the writers understood what they're getting into and that convincingly offered something others could comfortably buy into.

What's clear is that the true, or most profound, value of a business plan lies in the process of producing it rather than the deployment of the actual finished product. To do it right, the extreme entrepreneur must roll up their sleeves and delve into the minutiae of the industry and market segment of choice; then get down and grapple head-on with any and all strategic, tactical, and financial contingencies.

> What's clear is that the true, or most profound, value of a business plan lies in the process of producing it rather than the deployment of the actual finished product.

By the end, a totally focused EE should neither harbor nor put forth any illusions or delusions—except those, of course, that will help ensure a phenomenal success.

Location, Location, Location...

There's huge variance in the role a company's location plays. For many retail stores, for example, a physical street location is *the* key determinant of success. But for an e-commerce Web site or a catalog company with a cyber-location on the Internet, one's geographical zone of operation is irrelevant.

Finding an auspicious first site for a particular business is tricky. Ted Waitt didn't let an unlikely location deter him from creating a hugely successful company. His family's Iowa cattle farm served just fine for launching a mail-order PC assembling enterprise. Waitt even adopted a bovine moo-cow box motif as his *Gateway 2000's* trademark mascot. His juxtaposition of high technology and farm animals was a shrewd move— farmers are associated with solid American virtues, such as industriousness and reliability. This clever subtlety worked for Waitt.

Most entrepreneurs launch companies in their home vicinity, and move to larger premises or perhaps relocate when their business hits a certain stage. But some business ideas are inherently geographical, and site considerations are paramount.

When Fred Smith set out to create FedEx, for instance, location was anything but an arbitrary issue. The model he worked out was based on a hub-and-spoke transportation system, with integrated air/ground service. Smith knew that the hub/spoke model is tremendously efficient in large-volume frameworks—despite the apparent waste when you look at individual transactions in which a package takes an illogically long route to go from one spot to a close-by destination.

Also, from his experience in the service, Smith saw that the same company could effectively handle both trucks and planes, though these modes had always been run separately. While Smith didn't invent the hub/spoke idea, he was the first to apply it to cross-platform logistics.

Through exhaustive research, Smith determined that Memphis, Tennessee was the ideal spot for the national hub, as this location afforded good proximity to a large area of the country. But a suitable central location was just the beginning. The FedEx concept is a massive network, requiring huge upfront capital to create. Eventually, of course, with his solid business model and comprehensive business plan, Smith obtained the funding he needed. And FedEx got off the ground. Today, when it "absolutely, positively *has* to be there overnight," who do you think of?

Berry's Motown and Ben & Jerry's Moo-Town

Sometimes an extreme entrepreneur gleans so much benefit from a locale that honor simply must be paid. Berry Gordy, for example, had multiple reasons to call his company Motown Records. For starters, Gordy made the fullest possible use of Detroit's surfeit of black musical talent— of which he himself was a first-order star.

Wood Shingle, Cyber Shingle, or Both?

Until recently, picking a location for one's business just meant selecting a neighborhood or town you wanted to operate in. Or, if you were really planning big, like Fred Smith with FedEx, you thought nationally—or perhaps even internationally.

Now radio, TV, and the Internet have changed this for all time. For example, this year alone famed infomercial pitchman Ron Popiel will sell $225 million worth of Showtime Rotisserie ovens on TV—and all told, for the last few years, his sales for this one product alone will top $1 billion. Considering this is only one of numerous products that span decades of TV selling for Popiel, it is apparent he needs no physical "bricks and mortar" location to move his goods.

While this extreme hawker has proven the airwaves are as good a place to set up shop as any, new extreme entrepreneurs are bypassing TV and radio and heading straight for the burgeoning Internet and new global e-commerce with a potential for perhaps even greater success.

Why so? The numbers are mind-boggling. Web users around the world today number 300 million—and by the year 2005, it is expected to top one billion. A recent survey, conducted by Canadian-based Angus Reid Group, reports that in 2000 the U.S. led with 107 million personal computer owners, of which 60 percent are frequent and knowledgeable Internet users, with another 33 million expected to go online by 2001.

> **Web users around the world today number 300 million—and by the year 2005, it is expected to top one billion.**

Canada was next in line with regard to ownership and Internet usage, with Sweden, Finland, Australia, and Switzerland also considered to be leading-edge countries in computer usage and Internet literacy. Still, home computers and Internet usage pale when compared to almost every other type of consumer electronic communication device. Out of 28,000 survey respondents spread over 34 countries worldwide, 97 percent owned a TV, and 48 percent had a mobile cellular phone, while only 42 percent had a computer and only 20 percent had Internet access. (No wonder guys like Ron Popiel still reign supreme.)

The survey also showed a curious and growing fascination for handheld wireless Web-capable products like high-end pagers and Palm Pilot computers in Japan and many countries throughout Europe—often far outstripping the number of desktop

Both, continued

and laptop computers in use today. Thus, the U.S. model of Web access from a home PC seems destined for change—and both activity and resulting sales volumes generated are expected to be greatly impacted by this coming mobility and new anywhere convenience.

So, as the extreme entrepreneurs of today and tomorrow begin seeking out real estate in which to set up shop—they have many more options to choose from, including a "bricks and mortar" physical location, a vast national TV "on air" empire, or an Internet cyber-shop of unlimited global proportions (or any combination thereof).

It's food for thought, and as they say, "the times, they are a-changin'"—*fast*.

Gordy also took advantage of the low cost of producing music in the hinterlands of Motor City; and—for far less than the going rates on the two coasts—he turned out sounds that sounded as good, or sometimes even better. Despite his imperative to control costs carefully, Gordy launched a classy operation; call it "high-heel bootstrapping." In turn, necessity (which was the mother of invention) became the genesis of the sound—the *Motown* sound—that today still sets the pace for much of popular music currently being produced on both the right and left coasts.

> Sometimes entrepreneurs need to tie their geographical string to a different yo-yo than what they originally had in mind.

Sometimes entrepreneurs need to tie their geographical string to a different yo-yo than what they originally had in mind. When Ben and Jerry first were planning an ice cream operation, their initial idea was to plant the first shop in a warm-climate college town. But due diligence revealed that those target markets were saturated with the kind of shop they envisioned for their own.

So, in a deliberate application of contrarianism, the B&J guys inverted the paradigm and headed to upstate Vermont instead. Not only did it work out well, but also B&J's communitarian ideology meshed perfectly with Vermont's particular (agri)culture. Their insistence on using local (and mostly organic) farm goods became integral to Ben & Jerry's market identity and ultimate, resultant success. For many consumers, Ben & Jerry's popularity has little to do with ice cream itself but is instead represented by the company's much-vaunted and well-known commitment to progressive causes—and these consumers consistently "let their conscience guide their buy."

For many consumers, Ben & Jerry's popularity has little to do with ice cream itself but is instead represented by the company's much-vaunted and well-known commitment to progressive causes

If pressed some buyers of Ben & Jerry's products might even admit to preferring another brand of ice cream, but the fact that the Vermont company is committed to environmental activism and community give-back programs often decisively tips the scale competition-wise. (Of course, were it not for the fact that B&J *does* make a terrific line of ice cream delectibles, this moral aspect in all likelihood would melt into a moot...or *moo'ed* point.)

The Extreme Hard Facts

To a seasoned entrepreneur, many of these insights may seem basic and somewhat obvious. But in reality, they cover facts that are not to be ignored. Ever.

When a customer, a potential partner, or venture capital firm can select but one company with which to place their trust and money, why should it be yours? Your product, your persona, your dream is on the line. What will it take to put it on the *dotted* line?

Today and tomorrow, vast sums of money sit ready and waiting for the right message, the right product, the right plan—and the extreme entrepreneur who blends tried-and-proven techniques with new and fresh thinking will prevail.

In the end, it all comes down to asking questions. Simple questions, like: Is my product ready for the market? Do I have enough money to get started? And more extreme questions, like: How many ways can I infect the market with my off-the-charts enthusiasm for and confidence in the surefire success of my killer USP?

GASSING UP THE TANK
Capitalization

This all-important chapter begins by making one point crystal clear: money—in and of itself—is a strange breed of animal. Nearly 250 years ago Benjamin Franklin succinctly put the self-educating aspect of this commodity into proper perspective with this observation: "If you would like to know the value of money, go and try to borrow some." Indeed, this is the undeniable truth of attempting to raise capital for just about anything you choose to do on this planet.

No matter what you carry away from this chapter, or carry into any situation that involves a plea for money—remember Mr. Franklin's truth, and the above basis for what is the most common, most important, and perhaps most crucial cat-and-mouse game in the world: the quest for money.

Capitalization is the Big Kahuna of start-up issues—no matter how good your idea, you ain't goin' nowhere without at least some of that do-re-mi. Sure, there are start-ups on a shoestring, bootstrapped start-ups, garage

5

start-ups. And some of these are the most extreme ways to do it—witness the success of entrepreneurial giants like Bill Gates (Microsoft), Paul Orfalea (Kinko's), and the two Steves at Apple, who started with almost nothing more than their own fierce entrepreneurial creativity and drive to succeed.

But every entrepreneur is likely to need at least a little (if not a whole lot) of scratch to get the wheels in motion. How extreme you are is determined by how creative, nimble, and decisive you can be in the matter of capitalization.

If your goal is to float your boat and take a long, ambling, low-key ride down the entrepreneurial river, you can go at the capitalization thing any number of traditional ways—use your life savings, borrow from your family, get a bank loan, even take on investors. These are all reasonable, tried-and-true approaches for the average entrepreneur. The extreme entrepreneur, on the other hand, uses any and all of these techniques to gather seed funding, as well as an array of other, more hotdoggy tactics (that may involve selling his grandmother down the river).

Capitalization: Process or Event?

It has been said that love makes the world go 'round. Others claim that money is the ticket. For those who love money, they see no contradiction here at all. However, in reality the second is the truism that fuels our world. Money makes things happen.

One thing's for sure: starting and growing a business takes cold, hard cash. Sometimes not much—but at least some. Eileen Fisher borrowed from friends and family to get her first collection of clothes sewn, and when she couldn't borrow any more, she sold merchandise to acquaintances from her apartment. They paid wholesale, and got the clothes once they were actually made. Similarly, setting up in the folks' garage, investing loads of free time and just a few hundred bucks was enough for William Hewlett and David Packard to build from—but certainly, they still needed some operating funds to get under way.

One thing's for sure: starting and growing a business takes cold, hard cash.

Would *You* Lend You Money?

Asking this question of yourself is the first step for anyone setting out to secure funding for darned near anything. In fact, it is perhaps the key to maneuvering potential lenders into a positive mode that will produce successful results. The quicker you can say "yes" to this question, the better your chances will be with others.

At the next stage, once a lender decides to say yes, and that you are credit- or investment-worthy, a strange, near-universal phenomenon generally takes place. You will often find you have crossed a threshold of sorts, whereby you have shifted from (1) pleading your case, to a position where (2) the lender, now willing to make a commitment of cash, asks: "Will that be enough?"

> **Be realistic about how much you need to fuel up, and how much it will take to keep it running long enough to make a go of it.**

The point here? If they decide to go along with your request for capitalization, do not be surprised when a savvy lender—individual or institutional—checks to see if you have asked for enough. Meaning, will this amount just take care of the immediate problem or concern, or will it provide enough horsepower to truly end a crisis, break loose a log jam, or unleash momentarily stifled potential?

Be realistic about how much you need to fuel up, and how much it will take to keep it running long enough to make a go of it. Not unlike those college loans that followed you around like a hungry dog long after you got your degree, you don't want to be beholden to anyone for too much or too long.

Sometimes, it takes millions: famed extreme entrepreneur Fred Smith couldn't get his budding FedEx off the ground with just a wallet-ful of creatively maxed-out credit cards. Smith's thorough, detailed (and believable) business plan was his ticket.

More than most entrepreneurs, those considered to be extreme in their visions or ventures often must take (or have taken) creative and unusual approaches to enlisting start-up capital. These include, of course, those who are self-financed, or the bootstrappers (i.e., pull yourself up by the bootstraps). There are also the EEs who hit up only private networks of friends, family, acquaintances, and former business associates. And there are those who solicit outside capital, whether through government programs, angels, venture capitalists (VCs), or other institutional sources.

In pursuing outside investment capital at any level, extreme entrepreneurs frequently forget that the fanatical enthusiasm and persuasiveness—and groundbreaking nature of their EE venture—that works for them in some quarters, can cause potential investors to balk out of sheer caution. And justifiably so.

> The early-stage entrepreneur can't just focus on drumming up enough cash to get off the ground and then forget about upcoming looming fiscal requirements.

The early-stage entrepreneur can't just focus on drumming up enough cash to get off the ground and then forget about looming fiscal requirements for a while. A fast-growth company will quickly outgrow its capital structure; savvy businesspeople consider capitalization a *process*, not an event.

Thus, to avert "down the line" sure crises, any forward-thinking entrepreneur should also try to accurately project at least one year into the future to assess capital needs. Two years is even better—and smarter.

To Be (Flush) or Not To Be

There's ongoing debate over the issue of capitalization—specifically, whether it's better to start out with an abundance of funds or to cut your teeth with fiscal austerity. Now, you might be thinking "huh?"—who wouldn't want an excess of cash? Isn't that a no-brainer? Not really.

Advocates for the wisdom of abundance readily point out that a cash crunch is among the most common problems that torpedo young business start-ups. Confronted with a cash-flow crisis, a new entrepreneur's time and energy then must be diverted *and* devoted to raising funds—and often done so in a frantic manner that undermines sound business judgment.

Under such duress, relying on the goodness or profit-mindedness of strangers, the pressured EE is likely to concede a chunk of the business in return. But if the company has a healthy supply of money on hand to start with, unexpected rapid growth or operational needs won't trigger a mad scramble for more capital. As we said it's a wonderful concept and a virtual no-brainer....right?

Well...on the flip side of the issue are the "lean-and-mean" champions, who believe bare bones financing is actually preferable for fledgling companies, especially those in the extreme column. Accordingly, with little cash to throw at problems entrepreneurs learn to devise creative, frugal solutions, and are less inclined to be overly comfortable—or to squander resources, as is often the case when money is more plentiful.

Numerous business experts say they've seen more start-up business errors committed as a result of *excess* funds than those emanating from a cash-deficient situation. With just barely enough money to operate, entrepreneurs can't and don't avoid learning; with too much, though, or what might be considered plenty—or even slightly more than enough—it's tough to resist the easy outs.

> Countless business experts say they've seen more start-up business errors committed as a result of excess funds than those emanating from a cash-deficient situation.

As mentioned above, much depends on the kind of business you're building. An innovative "soup and sandwich" food concept may not need a huge bundle to get rolling—just as a hit with location number one may ultimately spawn a huge franchise opportunity and thus grow itself. But something like a serious bio-tech venture requires big bucks up front to purchase research equipment and supplies, and to pay scientists.

And yet...even when the demand is great, a determined EE can accomplish wonders.

Sometimes Trying Harder Is Enough

Warren Avis, for example, the tenacious extreme entrepreneur whose breakthrough innovation was coupling car rentals with air travel, started out with a relatively skimpy $10,000 of his own funds and a personal loan for $75,000 more.

Having found a niche unclaimed by Hertz, he began putting his car rental counters where it *counted*—right at the airport, versus off somewhere in town. He went after the leader at full throttle. With his keen marketing mind, versus tons of cash, Avis steered his business to the number two car-rental slot within only seven years.

Remember "We try harder?" He did, and succeeded. He continued fueling his accelerated growth by licensing ever increasing numbers of operations only in those cities with medium-size to major airports. Giant Hertz soon felt his presence.

The point here? Unless you already possess or can unearth a vast sum of cash, don't shy away from having to operate lean and mean for a while. In many respects, it's a good thing.

A Dollar-Fifty and a Dream

Tales of successful entrepreneurs who start with meager capital and then soar to stellar heights on wit and drive alone always have heroic

When It's Musical Chairs Time

Every so often, the entrepreneur's world of ready investment sources comes to an abrupt halt—albeit only temporarily—or perhaps the potential flow is slowed by any number of unforeseen economic events such as stock market flutters, rising interest rates, or nasty inflation (to name but a few culprits). At such times, EEs must tighten their belts and fundamentally change the way they do business and view raising money to survive. Here's what venture capital pros suggest:

- *Focus on profitability*. If you are to pique a VC or investor's interest in tight times, proving you can turn a profit within the next 12 months is critical. The "hang out your shingle and they will come" dot.com heydays of ready dough are a thing of the past. Solid business plans are now the order of the day. Reign in wild marketing expenditures. Also be realistic on projecting the cost of getting new customers, how long you think they'll realistically stick around, and what they're worth over the long haul. Without a clear picture here, you'll have trouble gaining a sympathetic VC or investor's ear.
- *Be urgent on raising cash*. Be realistic and do whatever it takes to succeed in a highly competitive market. Don't waste time dickering. Reduce over-inflated

Musical Chairs, continued

valuations for your company. The once-hot IPO market has cooled dramatically, and the majority of companies that had planned to soon go public have now pulled IPO plans and are pursuing other avenues. This goes for all types of companies, across the board—not just emerging dot.coms, e-commerce, and tech firms.

- *Pick new partners/investors with care.* Look for those who bring something to the table during troubled times—organizational know-how, a super track record, or lots and lots of cash are huge plusses. Nervous partners in nervous times is not a good combination. Pros with cool heads are your best bet. Dish out shares, titles, and board seats with care.

> Look for those who bring something to the table during troubled times

- *Go for more dough than you need.* If you do decide to raise outside money, set your sights a lot higher than just generating what you think you need now. It may dilute your ownership a bit more, but the additional funds will help weather what may be a long haul before the climate improves and you can entertain raising funds again. Experts suggest that going for a year's worth of operating capital is not unreasonable for uncertain times.

- *Creatively control your burn rate.* Control outlay like a miser. Hire multi-faceted personnel who can wear many hats. The smaller the company the more important their versatility becomes. Carefully weigh the merits (and costs) of rolling out new products and services versus refining and working to the max what you've already got in place.

- *Develop creative incentives.* The glory days of offering employees juicy run-away stock option deals in new cash-laden ventures are quickly evaporating. Most likely, you will now profit better over the long haul by brainstorming creative ways to reward, motivate, and keep employees in a less dynamic era. Involving them in developing alternative incentive programs that they think are attractive can be very effective.

These are key points every CEO needs to take into consideration when planning an extreme entrepreneurial mid-flight refueling, whether for a new or seasoned venture.

appeal. Indeed, there are plenty of bootstrap EEs who begin with only the most meager of means and succeed.

Sometimes their circumstances are, or were, *so* stark that to prosper at all virtually demanded an extreme gift. It's difficult to imagine a better example than that of Madame C. J. Walker, who had $1.50 with which to found a company that eventually made her the first African-American woman to become a self-made millionaire.

Born the daughter of slaves in rural Louisiana, and orphaned at seven, Sarah Breedlove (who later became Madame Walker) worked as a laundress to get by. With her meager earnings, Breedlove still managed to raise a daughter and send her to college. But at the age of 40, she looked at the probable scenarios for their future with great (and justifiable) apprehension.

Also, like many black women of her time, Breedlove had lost much of her hair to the ravages of caustic pomades used to straighten, or merely style, African-American hair. Then in 1905 she had a profound dream one night while she slept in which an elderly black man, unknown to her, proceeded to tell her what ingredients to combine that, when applied, would grow her hair back.

Skeptical to following his general directions, Breedlove mixed these ingredients and testing it on herself. In a short amount of time her hair amazingly started to return. Though other companies were selling effective hair-growth products by that time, Breedlove believed hers was substantially better. In 1905 she began selling her "dream," if you will, from door to door—quite successfully.

In 1906 she relocated to Denver with her new husband, Charles Walker, and with his urging set up a mail-order business for hair products, which began steady growth from day one. Her company soon grew to include a beauty school in Pittsburgh and offices in Indianapolis. By 1916 she employed over 20,000 people in the manufacture and distribution of her products throughout the U.S., Central America, and the Caribbean.

Like the Very First Time

Legendary British extreme entrepreneur Richard Branson has repeatedly demonstrated extremism in a vast number of ways, and at the heart of his burgeoning Virgin empire, sheer financial gumption has always been paramount.

As a teenager, Branson launched his first venture, a magazine, with about $4,000 he raised by soliciting ads for the publication—well before the magazine even existed. He repeated the feat with his next enterprise: a mail-order business for selling records.

Once Branson's magazine venture was up and running he (following his own natural and uncanny intuition) and placed an anonymous ad in his magazine for low-price mail-order records. The response was quick and massive. All well and good, except for one fact: he had no albums, and record companies and dealers were committed to foiling this type of no-frills sales channel. Fortunately for Branson, he located a storeowner willing to let him buy the albums at a friendly price with the pre-order revenues that were pouring in.

Branson's subsequent feats of smoke-and-mirrors derring-do eventually led to the existence of his humongous $400 billion empire, which has revenues generated from the 200 or so companies that his little non-magazine and faux mail-order operation wrought. While this is not an approach many folks have the stomach for, it *does* make one think seriously about the merits of sticking one's neck out a bit.

Branson's uncanny instincts worked side by side with his rule-bending approach to capitalization. For instance, every day you can be sure he thanks his lucky stars that on a whim, he changed the name of his original fledging little company from *Slipped Disc* Records to *Virgin* Records—"because we were virgins in *business*," he recounts—clearly knowing deep down inside that today there's no way that an airline dubbed Slipped Disc would ever fly.

Throughout his career, Branson developed and fine-tuned his own personal philosophy of branded venture capital. He managed to launch a hodgepodge of ventures that often became wildly successful businesses, mostly by leveraging the word "virgin."

In exchange, Branson usually gains controlling interest and embarks on wild opportunism that often drives up profits, which in turn becomes *another* success that makes the Virgin name even *more* powerful and more

Beam Me Up $cottie

Need to find ready cash to grow your business? Looking for venture capital? Want to connect with a savvy financial consultant for advice? The Internet has thousands of answers just a mouse click away. Here are just a few to get you started:

- **MoneyHunter** <www.moneyhunter.com> The online kin of the TV series MoneyHunt TV, this is a good place to start your search for financing.
- **Bankrate.com** <www.bankrate.com> Compare credit card deals by mouse clicks.
- **Garage.com** <www.garage.com> Hunt for venture capital and angel financing here.
- **Lending Tree** <www.lendingtree.com> Shop online for credit cards, even car loans, by filling out an application at this site. The application gets forwarded to participating banks, which get back to you with an approval and terms. It's a simple way to comparison shop for borrowed cash.
- **Vfinance.com** <www.vfinance.com> Here's a rich venture capital library, with plenty of links to venture capitalists with cash to invest.
- **GE Small Business Finance** <www.ge.com/capital/smallbiz/index.htm> General Electric lends millions yearly to entrepreneurs. Find out how to get your share.

Another great site for entrepreneurs to visit and check for potential funding avenues is:

- **Commercial Finance Online** <http://www.CFOL.com> Billed as the world's largest database of monetary sources and links to capital resources. It's a free site for businesses, with a vast database of commercial banks, investment banks, financial consultants, and venture capitalists. List your business, your plan, and your needs. Discussion groups by e-mail and educational information are available.

These sites are currently some of the best on the Web and will certainly educate you and get you headed in the right direction.

valuable for the next business target and ensuing round of negotiations. See the pattern here?

As you will see, once an extreme entrepreneur's dream begins gaining momentum it often becomes a brand of sorts, and a magnet that then draws money into a growing vortex of success. The once "seeker of capital" becomes the venture capitalist—only now lending primarily the momentum of their extreme entrepreneurial success to propel others' fledgling ventures.

Hef's Energizer Bunny

Another good modern example is Hugh Hefner, who got his ball rolling in 1953 by borrowing $600, with his furniture as collateral. The majority of the money went into buying the rights to reproduce color photos of Marilyn Monroe *au naturel*.

Hefner then ran his magazine concept by a number of newsstand wholesalers, and their positive response was his go-ahead to form a company, sell shares to family and friends, and arrange to put out a first issue. In the annals of publishing lore, *Playboy*'s ensuing rise in circulation is hard to beat.

Hefner went on to open a chain of clubs, several hotels, and two casinos (one in Atlantic City and one in London), host his own cable TV show, and become an icon for the American male's concept of the very good life.

But a few of his ventures went bust at the beginning of the 1980s, by which time explicit erotica options proliferated, and Hefner's rather over-inflated cultural presence started to diminish. Still—just $600 and nearly 50 years later—there's no denying, Hef made good on his bootstrapped promise to himself and his readers.

Money Grows on (Family) Trees

Family donations constitute an age-old springboard to entrepreneurship, and the EE league offers some fine examples. Texan real estate maverick Trammell Crow, for example, began his ascent to the top rung of mogul-dom by using his wife's inheritance to buy a modest warehouse in Dallas.

Richard Dennis, the man who introduced the "contrarian" approach to commodity futures trading, got his start with a $1,400 loan from his father and a few hundred bucks from a

> Family donations constitute an age-old springboard to entrepreneurship.

brother. At the time, he was too young to be allowed on the floor, so he sat on the side and directed his father to make his trades.

Wily and steel-nerved, Dennis soon was playing the inherently ultra-high-risk commodities futures market to the hilt. He raised the stakes even higher by developing an uncanny, undisciplined, and ultimately *wildly* successful approach to anticipating and capitalizing on trends. It triumphed to such an extreme degree that it is *still* being formally taught in hundreds of classes today.

Obviously, Dennis made a fortune. He also trained other traders in his methodology, and even founded a think tank. Probably his most significant breakthroughs, however, were to apply burgeoning computer technology to assess competing strategies—and to trade around the clock.

At the other end of the privilege spectrum are those entrepreneurs who seem to have silverspooned rather than bootstrapped their way to the top. While beginning with impressive financial horsepower, their feats of derring-do and extreme entrepreneurship are both legendary and not to be dismissed just because they were originally well-funded.

> At the other end of the privilege spectrum are those entrepreneurs who seem to have silver-spooned rather than bootstrapped their way to the top.

As noted earlier, where others may have felt comfortably positioned, and as a result squandered precious resources, there have been many examples of those who drove relentlessly as though fighting to remain solvent. Their quest became pursuit of a dream—and capitalization became a process, rather than an event.

Ted Turner's story is a good example. Another is Howard Hughes', who was still in his late teens when his father died and left him $500,000 in stock. Hughes' relatives thought the bequest should be handled by a voting trust until Hughes turned 21. He did not agree. Hughes argued in court that he could, and should, vote his own shares.

The judge found in his favor, but also urged the ambitious teenager to continue his education and seek assistance from older men in handling the money. Hughes nodded his assent, agreeing to do so—but inside knowing he had no intention of heeding the advice.

Hughes immediately showed himself to be a phenomenally driven and focused business wünderkind. He first expanded his late father's oil-drill manufacturing company and bought out his relatives' shares. He then went into the movie business, in which he prospered. Hughes was worth over $20 million by his mid-twenties.

In the meantime, he'd developed a fascination with airplanes and air flight. In true EE fashion, Hughes learned to fly, bought a small plane, began to tinker, and opened a plane rebuilding and repair shop. He also started to fly competitively, winning many of his air races. Hughes hit the headlines in 1938, when he piloted one of his own planes around the world. Other owners began to clamor for him to work on their planes, and so he opened a new business: Hughes Aircraft Company, which grew into a multibillion dollar giant, in large part by dint of defense contracts.

Hughes was far from finished, though. He started scouting around for an airline company, convinced that intercontinental travel was going to take off. Hughes found a small company, bought it for a mere $12 million, and modified its name, thus creating Trans-World Airlines (TWA). The industry experienced prolonged growing pains, but Hughes stuck by his TWA, eventually selling it for over half a billion dollars in 1966.

Still producing movies, and overseeing his bevy of companies—which included a separate military electronics corporation he started in the 1940s—Hughes moved into yet another business realm. He'd taken a shine to Las Vegas, which by the mid-1950s had only just started to bloom. Remember that Bugsy Seigel's initial Flamingo Hotel—the first in Las Vegas—opened in 1947, only a few years earlier.

Hughes started to buy everything in sight—casinos, hotels, and real estate. His enormous resources were instrumental in building the town into the global gambling and high-life mecca it is today.

The sad and sordid tale of Hughes' later degeneration is well known to most. But few realize how extraordinarily dynamic, risk-taking, innovative, and eclectically brilliant an entrepreneur he'd been at heart.

Digging into the inner thinking of almost every wildly successful EE, one inevitably finds they were profoundly influenced by the feats of another extreme entrepreneur who inspired them to follow suit in some fashion. The important message for the EEs of today and tomorrow is to study these dynamic pioneers closely.

Listen to their message, study their successes, learn from their mistakes—lest you find yourself working hard to reinvent a wheel that is already in place. Often, profound insights are yours for the asking.

What's Pluck Got to Do With It?

There's a little-known extreme entrepreneur who presides over the junction of risk-taking, innovation, and capitalization: Bill Bartmann, whose story seems nearly too far-fetched to be credible.

In essence, with no significant assets left to his name, this entrepreneur secured a small loan from a bank to which he already owed $1 million. Within six years, he was a billionaire.

In 1985, Bartmann's Muskogee, Oklahoma, business—Hawkeye Pipe Services Incorporated—shut its doors. Like a final chorus in a Merle Haggard country-western twanger, it had "done gone good-bye." Hawkeye was an oil rig pipe manufacturer, and when OPEC suddenly fell apart, crude prices plummeted and the company was swept away like a house in a flood.

With Hawkeye gone, Bartmann was left with about a million bucks of personally guaranteed debt, and he felt powerfully obligated to make good on it. Collectors were calling his home to demand payment, and most adopted a nasty approach. Bartmann did not declare personal bankruptcy and stiff his creditors. Instead, he set out to find a business venture that could make him *a lot* of money, and *fast*.

Bartmann saw a notice in the paper for an FDIC auction of bad loans from a failed bank in Tulsa. At first, the idea struck him as hilariously idiotic. But then, he got to thinking about it and decided to go—just for a look-see. He looked at the list of delinquent borrowers, with its annotations from collection agents, and realized that he too was one of these unfortunate souls, and that many, like him, would probably be glad to repay part or most of their debts when they could.

However, he added a twist of his own. Instead of becoming a mere collection agent like others before him—collecting a commission on any payments made—he decided instead to buy the loans outright, for two cents on the dollar, and see if he could regain enough of the defaulted debts to make it worth his while. Certainly, this was as risky as anything he could imagine, especially as it had never been done before. Would he be throwing good money after bad?

Girls Go for Green

Historically, most women-owned businesses are financed with personal savings or self-generated loans for start-ups or to fuel growth, and in this sector most venture capital per se comes from family and friends—and often other women.

However, as the number of these firms continues to increase steadily and dramatically, venture capital companies have begun taking note and are finally lending their official seal of approval—VC funding. Currently 38 percent of all U.S. businesses are owned by women—equaling about 9.1 million companies of varying size.

Today, venture capital companies shovel billions of dollars into both start-ups and existing companies for expansion. According to VentureOne, a San Francisco-based research firm, VCs invested over $48 billion in a record 2,559 U.S. companies in 1999. Still, only 187 of these recipient companies had female founders—or about 7 percent—indicating that only about 2 percent of all venture capital currently goes to women-owned businesses.

The result is that many woman-owned businesses struggle and are burdened with restrictive debt while a vast pool of venture capital goes elsewhere and into traditional channels because female EEs have not been actively pursuing VCs by simply pitching and presenting their needs.

> Currently 38 percent of all U.S. businesses are owned by women—equaling about 9.1 million companies of varying size.

Ah, but times are changing. The percentage of women now aggressively seeking VC funding is suddenly on the rise. As the nature of their businesses also changes—from staid and conservative endeavors (with little VC appeal) to more explosive and fast-growing engineering, communications, and Internet companies (now with some stock market potential and pizzazz)—the VC money boys are sitting up and taking notice too. Ka-ching.

Another recent survey of 50 venture capital firms and 235 women-owned businesses indicates the barriers separating the two—like the infamous Berlin Wall—will soon be history. It found that 75 percent of the VC firms that previously invested in women-owned companies would welcome making more new investments with other female entrepreneurs. Surf's up in the VC investment pool for all EE females—and perhaps it's time to dive right in.

For more information, contact the National Foundation for Women Business Owners <www.nfwbo.org> and Forum for Women Entrepreneurs <www.fwe.org>.

The first thing he needed was some operating capital, so he went to the American Bank of Muskogee, to which he was already a million bucks in the red, and asked for an additional $13,000 loan. Zowie! If there were a sweepstakes for gumption, Bartmann would have been set for life. Enter the power of sheer determination.

Once he explained his business proposition, American Bank—already greatly exposed—was somehow swayed and he managed to secure the sum. (This story probably could not happen in a large city.) Working from his kitchen table, Bartmann collected $64,000 on the loans he'd bought for $13,000—a 400 percent return. Amazingly, he *again* returned to the bank asking for an even larger sum, and got it. A few months later he had paid back about a quarter of a million dollars of his debt.

In addition to clearing all of his debt, Bartmann founded *Commercial Financial Services*, which has grown into the world's largest bad-consumer-debt repository, today with more than $7 billion in its ownership. Along the way, Bartmann had to relocate his business from Muskogee to Tulsa, Oklahoma to take advantage of the larger city's better opportunities and infrastructure. His company still has an astonishing profit margin, in some divisions as high as 48 percent.

One of the secrets to Bartmann's mind-boggling success with CFS is that collectors are trained to treat the indebted as clients, not as vermin. They're friendly, cordial, and businesslike. Bartmann never forgot how it felt when he was down…but not out.

Hard and Software Money

Even though funding for Internet hopefuls occasionally cools momentarily, these still are Net-delirious times when available capital for dot.com start-ups seems limitless. In fact, it's difficult to remember when prospective technology launches weren't so favorably received.

Looking back, Oracle cofounder Larry Ellison often recounts his team's travails in seeking funds in a much different era—back around 1976. At the time, the goal was to perfect and bring to market the industry's first commercial relational database.

With $2,000 of their own money, Ellison and three partners ventured forth with no outside funding. At that time, venture capitalists didn't even entertain requests by aspiring software companies as being serious or high-potential business ventures—focusing instead on the emerging hardware market and manufacturers. In those days, the legendary VCs of Silicon Valley only put dollars into what they could see and touch, and not into intangible concepts like software (which, as they would discover, was the fuel that made these wonderful hardware innovations spring to life).

Fortunately, as Ellison points out, software then (and perhaps now) is not a capital intensive business. Many companies, including Microsoft, have gotten started on a proverbial shoestring. It took the Oracle founders two years to develop the first version, and then Ellison himself spent five weeks installing the program and teaching the training course on site to the company's first client: the Advanced Technology Division of Wright-Patterson Air Force Base.

With this, the product took off—yes, like a jet—and Ellison began to build the multibillion-dollar relational database juggernaut. It didn't take long for his ferocious business *modus operandi*—generally termed "ruthless"—to earn great antipathy in the fast-to-develop relational database market.

In fact, Ellison and Bill Gates have come to typify the scorched-earth variety of extreme entrepreneur.

Believe It

The success of the extreme entrepreneur generally hangs and hinges on but a few basic principles:

1. You *can* build an incredible empire from meager beginnings. The stories you've just read, and others you soon will read are proof that from small acorns mighty oaks can and do grow.

2. Extreme entrepreneurs often shoot an arrow into the air—to fall, they know not where. But, once launched, each minor business success—that keeps a venture viable—must be carefully studied and used as a stepping stone to the next level of extreme growth. Waiting for a clear path is not always necessary; getting under way is.

3. Once under way, every day that you succeed you gain credibility and your name and product

> Waiting for a clear path is not always necessary; getting under way is.

gains value. Remember you are building a brand along the way, much like Virgin or Playboy has, and it soon becomes a strong bargaining tool in negotiating with others who believe they can prosper more quickly through an alliance and as a result of your pioneering and resulting success.

4. If you do plan to involve others at time of launch, be a communicator. Even a bizarre concept, if well organized and thought out, can be sold to others. There are countless stories of extreme entrepreneurs who found incredible support from unlikely quarters simply by being prepared—and not being afraid to ask.

While venture capitalists are generally the toughest audience to approach and win over, others—often thought to be even more difficult—are often the most receptive, if approached correctly, creatively, and effectively.

Bankers, investors, and potential partners are not above taking a flyer on an idea they think can win. Financial advisors of all types are a good sounding board, and they have incredible resources—and contacts—at their disposal.

The quest for investment capital is the ultimate challenge for the extreme entrepreneur. Make appointments. Meet with the enemy. Make your case. You may be surprised.

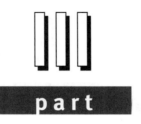

part

EXTREME SIZZLE AND SALES

Product. Marketing. Image. Sales. They can hardly be segregated as separate activities in modern business. The product and its positioning are inseparable. Marketing of the product intermingles, overlaps, and merges with imagery and sales in such complex weaves that in most cases there's no way to say where one ends and the other begins.

Throughout the history of business and commerce, extreme entrepreneurs have served to advance the art and science of marketing in every way. Product innovation cannot be effective without an accompanying and corresponding advance in positioning and marketing. Every step forward in sales in turn impacts company management and has marketing ramifications as well. And so the concentric circles of innovation—that begin as ripples—soon swell to gigantic waves that relentlessly pound against the shore of consumer acceptance and human progress.

While this is most obviously true for service industries, it also applies to produced goods. Because few products "sell themselves," even those "gotta-have" items or concepts still need to find their way to consumers and must be presented appealingly. Every element, from start to finish—company name, logo, the product, image, price, distribution channels, advertising campaigns, company policies—is a form of marketing and an opportunity to create or enhance sales. Each is also a point at which to get it wrong. That is, each marketing element is susceptible to misdirection.

Positioning is the distinct set of business processes that result in the creation of a welcome home for products in the mind of the buying public. When effectively executed, positioning flows naturally—like shimmering rivulets over smooth stones—from production to presentation and on to a warm reception.

Marketing is a vast subject, and I don't mean to suggest there's a disconnect between specific techniques and the long view of branding and other imagery considerations. But marketing is a verb and image is a noun, and we're going to take a closer look at the meaning of image—and the role it plays in the marketing mix later in this book.

While all marketing and image contribute to sales, these activities are not at all the same. In fact, it can be argued that marketing shouldn't be a standalone department at all. Some Japanese corporations, for example, have dissolved their separate marketing divisions, opting instead to instill the marketing as a *mindset* all throughout the organization.

Selling, unto itself, is a verb, however, complete with its own set of mechanics, skills, and know-how. The elite corps of entrepreneurs who are impressively extreme represent the embodiment and personification of the art of salesmanship. Radically so.

Marketing. Image. Sales. In the following three chapters, we look at these intriguing activities in all their intertwined, pervasive, and persuasive glory.

MARKET This!

Classic marketing is like Classic Coke™: familiar, friendly—a fixture, really. Extreme marketing is more like Jolt™, that insanely high-octane beverage that'll keep you up for three days straight. It's an edge and energy thing.

Let's take a moment to define the terms. Marketing is the process by which information about a product or service designed to meet a need (real or perceived) is conveyed to those who have (or perceive they have) the need. This process is usually a part of an overall business plan, but can also benefit from spontaneous actions or events.

Traditional marketing, then, is the process of finding and getting access to the market you've defined for your product or service. The goal of traditional marketing is to get your message in the hands of as many of your targeted, most highly motivated prospects as possible.

There are many tools and strategies used by the mainstream and extreme marketer alike. These tools can range from written communication with your market

6

chapter

(brochures, newsletters, direct mail, even a business card) to electronic info (Web site, e-mail) to broadcast (advertising, telemarketing, public relations campaigns, sponsorship of events). Your marketing strategy can even be inherent in many nuts-and-bolts aspects of your business, from location to distribution methods to customer service policies to pricing strategies.

Marketing in the last century has taken some extreme turns, in part because of modern influences such as radio, television, and the Internet. Once upon a time, a marketer looked for a market not much further than he or she could reach through personal, mostly local appeals. Call it Main Street marketing, the kind that existed when the barber or the grocer or the blacksmith needed only to communicate their products or services to their own neighbors.

> Marketing in the last century has taken some extreme turns, in part because of modern influences such as radio, television, and the Internet.

Then thanks to the advent of modern communication came mass marketing, the broadcast of the message to the widest possible audience, period. Throw out as many seeds as possible and something's bound to sprout. This saturation approach wore out its welcome, though, after creating decades' worth of clutter and a jaded and distracted public. It was not an ideal marketing scenario. So taking a swing back in the direction of personal, relationship-based marketing, the extreme entrepreneur has taken up some creative techniques for speaking to its market.

The Way of the Guerilla

Classic marketers are often number crunchers. They rely heavily on surveys, studies, and market research. They develop whole marketing machines—departments within their endeavors—to develop marketing plans, generally focused on targeted advertising campaigns.

Classic marketers also rely on the power of the brand, the product identity they forge and hope to lodge in the public's mind. Brand marketing is marketing in broad, obvious strokes—buy a bunch of advertising in

It's a Wild, Wired World

While it's still too early to easily determine which Net-repreneurs deserve to be classified as EEs, *the Net itself* is a de facto marketing EE. In a mere handful of years, the medium has inverted, subverted, negated, and mutated most of the established "rules" of marketing and business formation, and the process will no doubt continue, if not accelerate.

Today's marketing revolution is the result of countless human agents in collaboration with a startlingly "discontinuous" technology. The following outlines some of the more direct (and indirect) Net-mediated shifts in current marketing activities.

- *One-to-one printing, or "variable-data printing."* With computerization, marketing materials now can be easily personalized, not merely with the recipient's name in faux-handwritten script, but with content specifically gathered and particularized to a consumer's interests. This means less physical waste, and already dramatically higher response rates. As a result of targeted and informed marketing, industry research has shown increases of up to 24.5 percent in average order size, 36 percent in response rate, and 47.6 percent in repeat orders. This

> **Today's marketing revolution is the result of countless human agents in collaboration with a startlingly "discontinuous" technology.**

is a manifestation of Don Peppers' marketing notion: "Instead of selling one product at a time to as many customers as possible, the goal of the 1:1 marketer is to sell one customer at a time as many products as possible over the lifetime of that customer's patronage." Computerization and easy information gathering, or information provided by willing Internet customers, today create vast databases that are mined and honed to unearth more perfect and lasting product-to-customer matches than ever before in history—and sales figures, as those above, bear this out.

- *Permission marketing.* Seth Godin's increasingly familiar phrase and technique emphasis is based on marketing information *willingly* provided by consumers in specific product categories. This info, maintained by computerized databases (and fed by Internet ordering and usage) indirectly invites

Wired World, continued

a business (or like businesses) to re-contact the customer and to make similar offers that both sides know will be of interest. In an online, e-mail driven context, this can be a powerful tool.

- *Payment for reading/listening to ads.* This is an experiment predominantly born on the Web that may eventually die out, or at least continue to shift in form. It has given new meaning to the term "free," as it relates to everything from e-mail to telephone service. The heart of the premise is giving something for free in exchange for people being exposed to a barrage of advertisements. Unrelated banner ads on Web sites (often also with a direct link to the advertiser's site) were the precursors. Now it is spreading to non-Web applications as well—such as free telephone service, both local and long-distance, in exchange for a few moments of your time to listen to recorded advertisements before placing your call.

- *Information-rich marketing.* Consumers will have instant access to as much background information about a given product, category, vendor, or market as they care to glean. This changes the relationship between the parties. And misleading advertising or false propaganda becomes far more perilous to the purveyor. Computers, and the acclimation to instant access of information, are just a couple of the things driving today's smarter and better-informed consumers toward re-use of favored products with which they feel comfortable and have been previously satisfied.

- *Paying fans to promote on the Web: "Wired-of-mouth."* Or "word-of-mouse," if you prefer. This is another Net-inspired, or at least greatly rejuvenated, practice that may soon evaporate or vastly intensify. This falls under the viral marketing category, and enthusiasts are encouraged to tout their favorite products in exchange for their favorite goodies. Some call this "harnessing the buzz"—as apropos of the electronic beehive metaphor. The result? If successful, it could lower marketing costs and may create tremendous new opportunities for small and mid-size players to compete in a major way. Movie-wise, the recent runaway success of the solely Net-promoted, buzz-driven *Blair Witch Project*, succeeding against big studio releases, was a first—and a ready example of this awesome new marketing force.

These are but a few of the direct (and indirect) Net-mediated shifts available for EEs to currently ponder as new marketing trends and tools.

national media, and wait for people to buy your stuff. Nothing wrong with classic brand marketing—it turned Procter & Gamble into a cash machine, for heaven's sake.

This approach has reached a point of saturation, and fewer and fewer new attempts at big brand marketing hit their mark. So even the big guys have to get creative.

One of the first extreme ways entrepreneurs looked at the marketing challenge was to think like a guerrilla. Same kinds of products or services—but with new, aggressive, innovative ways of forging a relationship with the market. The guerrilla marketer shifted the focus from the volume of the advertising to the impact of the message, looking to reach ten people with a message that works effectively rather than 100 people with a message that doesn't.

> One of the first extreme ways entrepreneurs looked at the marketing challenge was to think like a guerrilla.

There's a lot of underground, hit-em-where-they-ain't surgical strike force this approach, and it's at the heart of all of the innovative ways extreme entrepreneurs have figured out to market their goods.

Going for the Jugular

The saga begins with a young California visionary name Michael Lajtay (pronounced Lay-tay). After completing business school and spending a number of years eagerly developing successful sports marketing programs for others, he sat down one day and said to himself, "Why not do this for myself instead?"

So in 1996, Lajtay developed a fiendishly simple yet powerful concept to enter, capture, and dominate a niche market in a blitzkreig fashion truly worthy of the label extreme entrepreneur.

Through previous business projects, friends, and personal lifestyle tastes, Lajtay had been thoroughly exposed to the young and unorganized—but growing—world of extreme sports. This included everything from skydiving, rock climbing, and bungee jumping to gravity sports such as snowboarding, downhill mountain biking, and street luge racing.

Lajtay knew there was a phenomenal market coagulating here, one quickly approaching critical mass. He knew this market could be identified and crystallized in a single word. In one inspired burst, it came to him: *Jugular*. To most, it might seem but a word, but to Lajtay, it was golden.

Jugular was unique and pliable, and the more he played with it, the better it became. By nature, it sounded edgy and extreme. It translated accurately and intact into the world's most commonly used languages. The more Lajtay analyzed it, studied it, and worked with it, the better it looked—and sounded. So he quietly went to work, first registering the name to protect it, then working up a plan.

A business school professor friend helped him craft a business plan, and upon completion, told Michael, "I'd like to invest in this." Which he did, to the tune of $60,000. So Lajtay had just enough seed money to progress to phase two.

Lajtay was now in full-battle mode to bring his word to life. He asked friend and renowned graffiti artist Mear—designer of hip MTV-type street artwork logos for everything from CD covers for Limp Bizkit to Fortune 500 products like Adidas™ and Coca-Cola™—to apply his talents in creating a distinctly extreme logo for Jugular.

After registering the logo in numerous fashions, Lajtay's first inclination was to investigate creating a line of clothing for extreme sports. But he quickly found it to be prohibitively expensive. Then he discovered the key to licensing, strategic alliances, and joint ventures and took a page out of Ralph Lauren, Bill Blass, and Calvin Klein's book (all of whom license the use of their names to other clothing manufacturers rather than producing their own lines).

Lajtay's second stroke of genius (after the Jugular name and logo) came in deciding to sponsor various hot athletes and teams in extreme sports. Suddenly, for very modest dollars, huge Jugular logos were everywhere—emblazoned on the legs, arms, chests, and equipment of extreme sport superstars in action. His word—his product—had met and become his niche market.

The result? Twofold: (1) Companies looking to get into the extreme sports world saw Lajtay's hip Jugular logo, and began discussing licensing deals to put it on their lines of clothes, accessories, gear, or whatever; and (2) all the adoring, wannabe extreme sports fans, wanting to emulate their heroes, began snapping up anything they could get their hands on with the Jugular logo.

At this point, it doesn't take much imagination to see how Lajtay's brainchild suddenly grew from decals and T-shirts to high-end clothing, and today to a wide and ever-growing range of everything imaginable—from Activision™ interactive games to Zippo™ collectible lighters.

Cutting to the chase, after only four years Lajtay has just returned from his second licensing show with a million dollars of contracts in hand for this year alone. And those just represent the base guarantee—the amount he will receive even if not one item is actually produced or sold bearing the Jugular logo. Not bad, when you consider all Michael Lajtay did was market one word: Jugular.

Buy This Book

Jeff Bezos and Amazon.com may be the finest example of marketing in the extreme. Amazon has successfully launched bold and original marketing initiatives that have been the cornerstone of its success—and which have redefined marketing possibilities for every entrepreneur that has followed. Bezos has got so much original marketing going on at Amazon it's hard to know where to start.

Let's see. He's got the *affiliate program*, the first of its kind, a low-cost, self-propagating technique that rewards outside parties for promoting Amazon's book site. For example, go to <www.cultivatedgardener.com>, an active gardening Web site associated with an upscale gardening show that airs on public radio. Gardeners love books, so the bookshelf on the Web site features many of them, either favorites of the show's host or those that have been featured or reviewed on the show. Each of these books is linked to Amazon. Say a million people use this gardening site in a year, and 5 percent of them (50,000) check out the bookshelf and just 10 percent of those people click through to Amazon and buy a book. Well, that's 5,000 book sales Amazon had to spend no advertising dollars to land. It merely has to reward the affiliated party for any effort in bringing in the sale.

> Amazon has successfully launched bold and original marketing initiatives that have been the cornerstone of its success.

Please and Thank You

Permission marketing is a concept explored and defined by marketing maverick Seth Godin. Permission marketing is based on the premise that mass-market advertising fights for people's attention by interrupting them. A commercial interrupts their favorite television show. A telemarketing call interrupts dinner. Print ads interrupt an article you are trying very hard to stay interested in. The interruption model is losing its effectiveness, mainly because people have learned to anticipate and ignore the interruptions.

> Permission marketing calls for the marketer to politely persuade consumers to volunteer their attention.

Permission marketing calls for the marketer to politely persuade consumers to volunteer their attention, to "raise their hands" in Godin's terms, and agree to learn more about a company and its products. By breaking the marketing of a product or service down into a strictly voluntary, step-by-step education process, the marketer opens the door to turn strangers (potential customers) into friends (friendly prospects) and friends into loyal customers. This approach takes the one-to-one thinking a step further, and builds in the prospect of deep, long-lasting relationships.

Some percentage of these sales are new customers, for which Amazon has paid a small fraction of what it would have paid to develop per customer in a traditional advertising and promotional marketing scenario.

Jeff Bezos has also revolutionized the *permission* aspect of his relationship with his customers (see sidebar above). Indeed, Amazon has taken great care in developing this asset, and it is possible that when all the dust settles—and Amazon gets out of those unwieldy, un-Amazonian businesses like selling kitchenware and power tools—Amazon's true value (and the potential for finally realizing a profit) may lie in its vast database of permission-driven relationships.

Here's how it works. Every time Amazon sells a product to a new user, it gains permission to speak to that user on subjects it now knows are of interest. So John Doe buys a book on the history of the U.S. Naval Academy. Amazon's database notes his product preference, and when a new book on an Annapolis-related theme comes out, Amazon has permission to make Mr. Doe aware of this new book.

"Dear Mr. Doe: As someone who purchased *Annapolis: A History*, you might be interested in knowing about a recently published book called *The Future of the American Naval Tradition*. You can order this book at a savings of 30 percent by following the link below..."

John Doe may or may not buy the second book, but eventually he will buy something new as a result of Amazon paying attention to what he likes and kindly letting him know when something of interest is on the horizon.

Thanks to the immediacy and seeming intimacy of e-mail, this feels like a mutually beneficial personal relationship to John Doe. At an amazingly low cost to Amazon, it is building a highly valuable, long-lasting relationship that allows it to ask for this customer's attention again and again. It's a method that is radically far afield from big, broadcast, mass marketing but extremely contemporary (leveraging new technology to the hilt) and extremely effective.

Finally, Amazon has created an environment where customers are actively encouraged to review the products they've bought, and as a result there exists a thriving and powerful community of customers who market to each other. In essence, Amazon's saying, "Hey, we're all booklovers here, so let's talk books!" The more a customer feels his or her opinion is valued (the review is right there on the book's page, next to the book summary, for all the world to see), the more valued as a customer the consumer feels when ordering more books.

In addition, this mass quantity of customer opinion acts as marketing information straight from the market *to* the market. While the book's publisher or Amazon might not "market" a book by saying, "This book stinks!," the way an unfavorable customer review might, the fact is the more people talk about the books—*however* they talk about them—the more books they buy.

The community factor can be big. Done well, it can massively leverage the customers' knowledge to generate endless new business. Look at eBay. Community identity and intra-community marketing is at the heart of eBay's phenomenal success, and you can't argue with that.

Amazon has all sorts of other marketing initiatives at work, too, including plain, old-fashioned customer service. Customer service as a marketing ploy? Yep. By bending over backwards to keep each customer happy, they make the customer a loyal, repeat offender. Jeff Bezos considers Amazon's "anal-retentive, obsessive-compulsive" attention to the customer the secret to the company's customer growth, and a keystone to its overall marketing message. This is *not*, however, an inexpensive marketing tactic.

When Amazon's special pre-order promotion of the much-anticipated fourth Harry Potter book went awry, and thousands of customers did not receive their pre-paid copy of the book on their doorstep by Fedex, as promised, the day after the book was published, Amazon spent a fortune making it up to disappointed customers. They sent elaborate apologies almost immediately by e-mail. They sent gift certificates and reimbursements for shipping and in some cases gave the book to the customer for free. It wasn't the mistake that was expensive; it was the lengths to which Amazon had to go to maintain its marketing message that broke the bank.

Okay, I'll stop here about Amazon, but you see why it is a killer laboratory for extreme marketing techniques. Next!

Extreme Freebies

It may be a golden oldie of a marketing tool but when it works, it works in the extreme—I'm talking about branded promotional products, the free giveaways that are a perennial favorite of consumers. For example, when it first appeared in 1876, Anheuser-Busch's Budweiser beer was a premium product that had the rare advantage of retaining its flavor well for long periods once it had been pasteurized and bottled. The drink was distinguished from other beers by its natural carbonation, the result of a double-fermentation process known as *kraeusining*.

> It may be a golden oldie of a marketing tool but when it works, it works in the extreme—branded promotional products.

Due to the brew's resultant preservability, the company built Budweiser into one of America's first nationwide brands. Junior partner and salesman Adolphus Busch, an outgoing, charming man, traveled around the country to promote his company's quaff, leaving several salesmen in his wake to take orders.

But to instill a longer-term recollection of the taste experience, Anheuser-Busch distributed an assortment of decorative memorabilia: trays and posters emblazoned with "Budweiser Girls" (a technique still used today—only via live appearances), as well as copies of a lavish painting commissioned by the company, named "Custer's Last Fight," for customers to hang on their wall, among other memorable (and now collectible) knick-knacks.

By the turn of the century, the St. Louis Anheuser-Busch brewery was the country's largest, and Adolphus Busch was among the nation's wealthiest men, leaving a personal fortune of about $60 million upon his death in 1913. Fast forward to a century later and the Budweiser logo enjoys more fun in the sun during college spring breaks (on towels, t-shirts, banners, umbrellas, and other such items) than the rest of us will in a lifetime, hammering home the product's marketing message to its dream demographic.

Changing Horses Midstream

Sometimes the premium itself becomes so popular that it overtakes the original product and becomes the main event. Such was the case of William Wrigley, Jr., who owned a small, Chicago-based baking-soda company.

As he made his rounds, Wrigley promoted his product by distributing premiums such as cookbooks and toiletries with his goods. After making a deal with a local chewing gum manufacturer, Wrigley began to include two sticks of gum with each baking-soda order sold. When he started receiving requests in the mail to purchase the gum by itself, the budding EE recognized that opportunity had just knocked on the proverbial door.

> Sometimes the premium itself becomes so popular that it overtakes the original product and becomes the main event.

Not only did he discontinue vending baking soda, but he began to award valuable premiums to stores that bought sizeable orders of his chewing gum: free cash registers, office coffee makers, handsome display cases, and so on. Wrigley's intention, of course, was to influence the store owners with these substantial goodies to promote his gum over any and all competing brands.

A great believer in the power of direct marketing, Wrigley in 1915 assembled all the phone books in the country and mailed four sticks of gum to every subscriber—1.5 million people. By 1919, when he ran this same promotional campaign, the total subscriber base had grown to seven million.

Free introductory extreme marketing of this pennies-per-product single idea brought him untold wealth and a business empire that thrives to this day. Chew on that for a while.

Providing a Starter Kit

Around the turn of the century, King Gillette invented the safety razor thinking it might help to support his dream of being a writer and social reformer of the day. His first sales were made in 1903, when he sold 51 razors and 168 blades. He wasn't breaking any records with numbers like those, so he kept fiddling with price and positioning.

Gillette's ultimate stroke of marketing genius came with World War I, during the period from 1914 to 1918. As the doughboys packed up and shipped out to do battle "over there," Gillette gave each and every one a free safety razor to save room in their "old kit bag," as the song goes—and the U.S. government readily complied by purchasing scads of replacement blades.

When the war was over, the soldiers returned home and continued to use the trusty Gillette safety razors they had carried from trench to trench, and had hauled back with them halfway around the world.

In the 1920s, Gillette furthered this concept of strategic freebies, with countless promotions where razors were given away free to promote the on-going sale of replacement blades. Time and time again, Gillette plowed profits back into the business and expanded his cutting-edge marketing concepts worldwide.

When Gillette died in 1931, he held assets in excess of $60 million—an amazing fortune at that time. He also revolutionized the way men shaved. It was an amazing, extreme feat that impacted the daily life of about half the people on this planet. (And let's not forget women's razors!)

The Price Is Right

One of the most intriguing modern iterations of this "give away the razor and sell the blade" marketing technique is, of course, Internet driven. There's a thriving culture of technology business lenders who believe that the best way to market and create value for their product is to give it away for free.

The original leader of this tribe of thinkers is Brian Behlendorf, who banded together with seven other Web pioneers to create the Apache HTTP Server Project, the most popular Internet-server software in the world. Apache is an organization with no headquarters, no CEO, and no advertising. Its product, which ultimately was the integrated effort of hundreds of volunteers—and is absolutely free—has a market share of 50 percent, and provides the juice for the Web sites of big broncos like McDonald's, Sony, and the FBI.

> There's a thriving culture of technology business lenders who believe that the best way to market and create value for their product is to give it away for free.

That's cool, but if the product's free, how does it make any money? Apache has created a profit opportunity for a whole bunch of companies (*not* Apache) and products with actual price tags that supplement the Apache server; there's a more security-oriented adaptation of Apache that sells for a thousand bucks, and a version for the Mac that sells for half that.

Then there's Network Associates, Inc., the California-based company that is the world leader in anti-virus software development, controlling 40 percent of the market. How'd it become top dog in this category? By giving away its core products to gain market share. By the time it had 25 million users, and a whole range of ancillary products, they were charging for their stuff; they now enjoy a market cap of $3 billion.

This approach is very daring and hinges on the belief that if you build it *well*—and give it away for free—they will come in droves. And then you can make money. It's not a marketing ploy that suits every product or personality, but certainly extreme.

Ah-Choo!

Thanks to Amazon and others, affiliate or associate programs are one of the hottest self-perpetuating marketing initiatives going. These sorts of *viral* efforts are the tools of some of the most successful—and extreme—Web-based marketing applications. Going viral boils down to getting someone else to spread your message and drive visitors to your site (or your product). This used to be known as plain, old-fashioned word of mouth, but now it has some unique and high-tech twists.

> Going viral boils down to getting someone else to spread your message and drive visitors to your site (or your product).

Take Hotmail, for instance, one of the first, best practitioners of viral marketing. If you don't know what Hotmail is, it's because you don't have it, and if you don't have it, it's because no one ever sent a piece of e-mail to you via free e-mail server Hotmail. What's Hotmail's USP? Free e-mail. How do they market this USP? Well, this is one of those twists of entrepreneurial fate.

Extreme entrepreneurs Sabeer Bhatia and Jack Smith hatched their free, Web-based e-mail scheme in 1996, and took it to VC firm Draper Fisher Jurvetson, who immediately tossed $300,000 into the start-up's kitty. They also threw in the idea for self-referencing promotion for good measure. DFJ suggested a hot link at the bottom of each piece of free e-mail transmitted that read something like: "Get your free e-mail at Hotmail." This clever, trailblazing technique worked in spades; every outbound message conveyed an advertisement and an implied endorsement from the sender. By turning Hotmail's core subscribers into their own highly effective salesforce, Hotmail grew a subscriber base faster than any company in the history of the world, signing up 12 million subscribers in its first year and a half. This was at the bargain-basement cost of less than half a mill for marketing, advertising, and promotion. Sheesh. If they give away the e-mail service for free, then how do they make money? They amass a 12 million subscriber base, sell banner ads, then sell the company to Microsoft for a wheelbarrow-ful of money.

Other all-star viral marketing pioneers include Marc Andreeson and Netscape, who may have been the first to incorporate that "spread me"

EE Superstar: Scott D. Cook

If you're one of the 19 million people now using computer software by *Intuit* for your desktop computer, it might pay you to stop for a moment and ask: why? Because it's exactly how Intuit founder Scott D. Cook brought it to your PC or Mac in the first place.

While you ponder exactly what Intuit software is, let us say: 11 million now use and depend on the company's first brainstorm, *Quicken*, introduced 16 years ago to better manage personal finances. Another 4.2 million utilize its *TurboTax* prep software to grapple with the IRS, and 2.8 million more (individuals and small businesses) employ *QuickBooks* for day-to-day accounting chores. Nearly two million faithfully use two or more of these programs daily. Again: why? Better yet: How did this happen? Were Bill Gates and the folks at Microsoft sleeping at the switch? Perhaps.

Prior to 1984, Scott Cook was a fairly typical, happily married, mid-level executive for Procter & Gamble, and then later worked as a consultant for Bain & Company (a corporate strategy firm) as an expert on the ins and out of banking and technology. But soon his unique blend of business expertise— along with simple awareness and curiosity, common sense, and daring—galvanized with a flash of brilliance that ultimately put revolutionary new and simple "make sense" finance solutions on millions of hard drives.

> If you're one of the 19 million people now using computer software by *Intuit* for your desktop computer, it might pay you to stop for a moment and ask: why?

This incredible success story had very humble beginnings. It all began at the Cook's home kitchen table, where Scott watched his wife struggle with simple accounting chores. Later discussing this with his computer whiz friend, Tom Proulx (a programmer and then student at Stanford), they questioned if there might not be a better way to handle everything from paying bills and record keeping to balancing the family checkbook.

While Proulx went to work on the mechanics of programming a viable technical solution, Cook began by crafting a marketing strategy based on those used by Procter & Gamble for a wide range of consumer products. Their marketing was maddeningly simple and unbelievably successful.

Cook, continued

First, they watched. What were people grappling with? Where did they need the most help? They launched broad telephone surveys that helped tailor easy-to-use programs that people really wanted. When the first Beta prototype versions were ready for testing, Cook and Proulx actually followed users home to sit and watch them use it—making needed corrections, to simplify or improve, as problems surfaced.

Further, they asked questions in focus groups—and labored long and hard to produce simplified instructions written in plain English. Where computer eggheads before had taken pride in confounding we poor mortals with their cyber-prowess... Cook and Proulx took pity—making things understandable and easy-to-use—and everyone profited (especially Cook and Proulx).

> **Cook and Proulx first successfully blended common-sense and cutting-edge technolgy to create something we all needed.**

The final *coup de grace*, which set Intuit apart from other software purveyors of the day, was the industry's very first direct response television advertising campaign extolling the simplicity of *Quicken*, and—if you think back—it's probably what originally piqued your interest, got you to check it out, and had you plunking down the bucks for this wondrous new tool.

Cook and Proulx first successfully blended common-sense and cutting-edge technology to create something we all needed. They then used even clearer vision to carefully tailor it to and for us, with usability testing (five full years before anyone else), rather than vengefully forcing us to reinvent ourselves just to be able to use it. Finally, when it was ready, they advertised via the same medium we already used to find better brands of soap, new cars, and convenience fast foods.

Fiendishly simple, and incredibly successful, Intuit produced huge sales and incomes that now keep Scott and Proulx busy at their PCs. No doubt they are using their Quicken software just to keep up with the rich rewards of blending conventional low-tech marketing with hi-tech cyber-solutions wrapped in an easy-to-use/easy-to-understand presentation. What a concept!

Got a great idea cooking at your place? Don't lose it on the way to market. Make sure end users can grasp the vision just as clearly as you do. In other words, remember to KISS: "keep it simple (for) success."

feature in his product. Netscape's diminutive "Designed for Netscape" icon was quickly adopted as a status symbol by legions of Webmasters who used the logo to send the message that their site was cutting edge in Web-page design.

Then there's Amazon (again), whose affiliate program is a holy grail to would-be viral marketers; Yahoo!, which copied Hotmail's model to great effect; Pierre Omidyar's eBay; and Dave Bohnett's online community-driven Geocities, to name a few. Obviously your product's got to possess an element that lends itself to the viral approach. This doesn't mean it works for only products or services with an online component, but it sure helps.

Taking It to the Street

There's an extreme twist on marketing that's particularly effective when you need to create a buzz and immediate, grassroots momentum. It's called *street marketing*, and it works especially well when you're trying to get a product in the hands and on the lips of trendsetting young people.

Needing to make its presence known to influential young music afficionados, urban music and culture magazine *Vibe* decided to skip broadcast advertising as a model and go right where their audience could be found: on the street. *Vibe*'s "Street Teams" take cool *Vibe* stuff—stickers, CDs, magazine samples—to the top turf in the top markets where they want to influence and cultivate their audience. The Street Teams, which consist of three to ten members, seek out *Vibe*'s demographic, and cultivate visibility and brand identification right there on the spot.

There's an extreme twist on marketing that's particularly effective when you need to create a buzz and immediate, grassroots momentum called street marketing.

This targeted, cost-effective strategy has worked for *Vibe*, which claims it has learned as much about its market as its market has about *Vibe*, which ain't a bad add-on.

Love the One You're With

Sometimes the extreme entrepreneur's greatest—and most extreme—strength as a marketer is being nimble. It is a rare gift from the gods to have the opportunity to rethink and redirect a product to a different market, and see this new application go through the roof without a great deal of hoopla or initial advertising dollars.

> Sometimes the extreme entrepreneur's greatest—and most extreme—strength as a marketer is being nimble.

If there's one extreme entrepreneur who went where no entrepreneur had gone before— and to whom an entire species can feel grateful—it's Ed Lowe, who reaped a true windfall of secondary profits for his trouble. In fact, he is a perfect example of Edison's famous 1 percent inspiration and 99 percent perspiration definition of genius.

Lowe worked with his father in a sawdust business in Cassopolis, Michigan. One day in 1947 he overheard a friend griping that the sand and sawdust method she was using for her house cat just wasn't cutting it; it was messy *and* her house still stunk. At that moment, Lowe had a brainstorm.

The shop kept large bags of powdered clay around for sale to businesses and homeowners to soak up grease. Lowe was well aware of its legendary absorbency, and so did a little experimenting, and was soon satisfied with the results. He proceeded to test market his "new product" in five pound brown bags with the phrase *Kitty Litter* scrawled on the side. Naming accuracy and simplicity played a big role in Ed's success, as well.

Early on, Lowe had hardly enough money to fill his gas tank and travel the territory plying his wares. Certainly, no one took his enterprise seriously enough to even consider extending a loan. Gradually, however, things took off, and he eventually found a young banker willing to take a chance on this extreme entrepreneurial venture.

Kitty litter indeed. In the end, Lowe created a billion-dollar industry, and helped establish the cat as America's most popular pet. According to *People* magazine: "In the history of cats, there are two dates of significance:

1500 B.C., when the little creatures were first given shelter inside Egyptian homes, and 1947, when they finally became proper house guests, thanks to Ed Lowe."

Target versus Shotgun

The following chapters look at many other EE superstars—their approaches and successes—to glean insights as to what unique twists made their particular efforts in image development and sales extreme. For the moment, do remember that finding customers for your USP—whether a tangible product, a free service, or just a word—is, in reality, no different than seeking a job.

In the simplest of terms, traditional marketing theory would call for sending your resume to every company in the United States—and hoping one would bite. That's an expensive and labor-intensive process at best. Traditional *target* marketing would call for narrowing the field a bit with some research, ferreting out the best prospects, and mailing only to those you felt were a potential match, and so on.

Extreme marketing calls for picking but one: either a talent, a concept, or a product innovation that becomes a *unique selling proposition* that is yours and yours alone. The idea is to then apply it effectively in a particular market where it can and will shine. All of which paves the way for legendary *imagery* and ultimately scores *sales* that are earned—not bought.

IMAGE AND
the Public Eye

et's get one thing straight, right off the bat: image is every-thing. Whoever said it first certainly captured the essence of a very modern, if highly cynical truth: it doesn't matter who you (or your product or your company) really are, it's how you are perceived by your market that matters.

Look for a moment at the actual meaning of image and the difference between image and identity, and what that difference may mean to the ultimate recipient—your customers.

Webster's Dictionary defines identity as "being one's self or itself, and not another." Other examples include "what a thing or person is," "exact likeness," and so on. In 20 or 30 words, this concept is clearly and succinctly stated.

Conversely, only a few pages away, Webster uses nearly 1,000 words in an attempt to pin down image with explanations that range from "a likeness or repre-sentation of a person or thing," to "the general or

7

conceived public perception of a company, public figure, etc. created by careful calculation aimed at creating good will."

Obviously, creating image is the trickier and more complex concept of the two. Why? Identity is rather cut and dried. It is who you really are and what you are really all about. No baloney. Image on the other hand, is that which you would *like* people to believe. It is the façade you create, and the impression you project out at the world.

Taking this whole definition exercise one step further, corporate or product identity is reflected in the name and the logo, and this is executed in packaging, advertising, and every other way a company telegraphs its presence to the world.

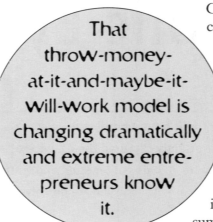

That throw-money-at-it-and-maybe-it-will-work model is changing dramatically and extreme entrepreneurs know it.

Corporate or product image is how the company or product is perceived in the marketplace. Companies spend billions trying to control that perception by sending messages out to the market that will (they hope) lock the desired perception in place.

Ha! Why am I laughing? Because that throw-money-at-it-and-maybe-it-will-work model is changing dramatically and extreme entrepreneurs know it. The fact is the vast majority of consumers hear about a company or product from another consumer, not from the company itself—and *what* the consumers hear from other consumers about your stuff *is* your image.

Take Volvo. Do you think those folks at Volvo sat around a table and decided in advance that they were going to be known as the "super-safe family car"? No, they built a distinctive car with some notable functions, and sent it to market. The car-buying community got to talking amongst themselves and before long, one of those word-of-mouth, grassroots, consumer-to-consumer marketing campaigns that was talked about in Chapter 6 had broken out. The *people* declared the Volvo the family-safe car, and now Volvo had an image, a highly marketable image, that they've proceeded to leverage for all it's worth. *Is* the Volvo the safest family car on the planet? It doesn't matter—that is its image.

Finding Your Place

On his 70th birthday, famed playwright George Bernard Shaw (1856–1950) was asked to comment on some early writings in his career, that were, well, unsuccessful, (i.e., real stinkers that never got published). Bemused, Shaw reflected back—and dismisses these setbacks as being mere literary growing pains. Then he added a few profound thoughts worth recounting:

Truth is, all men are in a false position in society until they have realized their possibilities [potentials] and imposed them on their neighbors," he noted. Then Shaw went on to add, "They are tormented by a continual shortcoming in themselves—yet, they irritate others by a continual overweening. This discord can only be resolved by acknowledged success or failure...and everyone will be ill at ease until they have found their natural place, whether it be above or below their birthplace.

I have constantly dinned into the public's head that I am an extraordinarily witty, brilliant, and clever man. That is now part of the public opinion of England; and no power on heaven or on Earth will ever change it.

So from his comfy perch in his sunset years, Shaw admitted he'd invented his image (his product), foisted it on his public, and then honed it to perfection. A lesson for the extreme entrepreneur. (Of course, it always helps to be a genius.)

Image versus Marketing

The relationship between extreme entrepreneurs and image has taken many turns and worked on many different levels. One of the most interesting and instructive scenarios involves the EE directly participating in the image process.

In some cases, the business identity is associated with the EE's personality—directly, as with chicken king Frank Perdue or Herb Kelleher, or indirectly, as with Christos Cotsakos (E*Trade) or Steve Jobs. In some cases, the EE is directly focused on the image dimension—such as Honda with the naming of the Acura.

For example, in Frank Perdue's case, the approach was to transform his distinctive looks, with his prominent nose and conspicuously bald pate, into a mock-aesthetic virtue that reflected on his product. One well-known ad features a photo of a proud-looking Perdue, which is captioned: "Baldness. Handsome in a man, beautiful in a Chicken." The product became associated with the man: folksy and wholesome, and button-popping-proud of it. An image is born.

John Delorean's advertising featured the dapper EE posing informally next to the caption, "Live the dream." And for the Delorean's bright, shining moment as the hip, dashing car of the future, the image was there. Unfortunately, Delorean wound up living 10 to 20 in the grey bar hotel, making license plates rather than automobiles. Still, it's excellent example of presenting and selling an image.

Baby, Baby, Baby!

In the case of Gerber baby food, the smiling, cuddly baby image successfully projected warmth and goodwill, and in turn sales, and eventually market domination.

Dan Gerber's pioneering efforts that created a mass market for baby food included several brilliant marketing ploys. First, the company promoted itself as "baby experts," by publishing a series of booklets on various aspects of infant upkeep. This went a long way to establish the brand's image as safe and authoritative.

Later, as a mild-mannered promotional ploy, the Gerbers posted a contest in which artists were asked to submit images of healthy babies, with the winning image to then be used as a pictorial logo, or mascot, on Gerber packages. One of the submissions was an unfinished drawing, and the image was so disarmingly pure and sweet that it became the "Gerber baby." It is unlikely that the Gerbers imagined this outcome, but it certainly secured the product's image for generations to come—that is, until the glass-in-the-baby-food debacle threatened to destroy years of positive image building. But more on reversing an image misfortune later.

Celebrity Yin and Yang

Over the past decade or two, entrepreneurs have supplanted politicians as objects of fantasy and interest. Entrepreneurs have the integrity of actually accomplishing something while politicians increasingly have come to be seen as mere pawns in the fists of powerful interests.

EE Superstar: Leo Burnett

Let's a look at one of the most innovative superstars of advertising, another key form of imagery. It is often said that when business is good it *pays* to advertise; when business is bad you've *got* to advertise.

Major league players in the advertising game concern themselves with little except image. But the extreme emphasis on visual manipulation is a fairly new development, and it's the result of one man more than anyone else: Leo Burnett.

Along with David Ogilvy and J.Walter Thompson, Burnett was truly a driving force within today's high-tech advertising industry. The creator of the Jolly Green Giant, the Pillsbury Dough Boy, and hundreds of other avatars of "consumer culture," Burnett shaped the collective psyche in his way nearly as much as Walt Disney did. Burnett pioneered the concept of mindshare, and proceeded to prove he was the great manipulator.

Before his ascendancy, words were the coin of the realm. David Ogilvy continued to develop the elegant, reasoned, respectful approach to hawking wares. But Burnett went straight for the pituitary.

He realized that an image is worth a thousand words, particularly when subconscious coercion is involved. Burnett didn't need to delve into Freudian theory to comprehend how TV was the ultimate weapon of subliminal suggestion, a visual medicine dropper dispensing suggestive images into our minds dozens of times a day.

> It is often said that when business is good it pays to advertise; when business is bad you've got to advertise.

As Burnett himself said, "Television is the strongest drug we've ever had to dish out." Burnett's approach was to isolate the essence of a given product, a quality that viewers must associate with the item to establish the soundest consumer connection. Next, devise a visual trigger that will rally the appropriate emotions to enforce the connection. The Marlboro Man is perhaps the most memorable visual cue Burnett created.

Despite its effectiveness in his lifetime, his approach was even more forward-looking, as it's come to underpin promotional techniques throughout our society. The use of sound bites, reliance on typography rather than text, removing the work the consumer used to have to do in order to make a decision—all are trends implicit in Burnett's methodology.

His ads sprang forth during an era of public innocence, relative idealism, and clear blue skies. He helped obscure any dark, cynical, or dangerous applications of heavily weighted and controlled imagery that loomed on the horizon.

As a result, entrepreneurs have come to occupy a higher-profile role in the public consciousness than they have since early in the century. This presents both great opportunities and formidable challenges. Ben Cohen and Jerry Greenfield are ideal icons of their company's image—its product, philosophy, and market placement.

> As a result, entrepreneurs have come to occupy a higher-profile role in the public consciousness than they have since early in the century.

However, the danger in possessing a strong, recognizable image is the imperative to maintain it. Any slippage will be especially conspicuous, because the public has been encouraged to blur the distinction between image and actuality. If Ben & Jerry's had announced a contract to become the sole supplier of ice cream to the Pentagon, for example, the company's public persona would be shot down or explode in mid-air.

A company's "personality" is often a projection of its owners' personality—especially when the founders are *truly* extreme entrepreneurs. Both internally and externally, in corporate culture as well as community relations, an organization reflects the style and values of its creators. This association often diminishes over time, but quite slowly. The picture is further complicated by the intertwining roles of the media and the PR machine.

If Not a Celebrity Yourself, Buy One

Because of their ubiquity, celebrity endorsements seem like an obvious marketing ploy. But like every other "natural" business move, someone had to think of it a first time, or rather think of it and follow up a first time. And that person was Albert Goodwill Spalding, one of the country's great baseball pitchers and a legendary extreme entrepreneur.

After the ball that Spalding had made for his own use was adopted as the official one by the National League in the 1880s, sales at the sporting goods company he and his brother owned and soared. Spalding then came up with the idea of paying star players to permit their signatures to appear on equipment items.

This marketing technique was a very big hit, opening another path for Spalding's future triumphs. It was also the beginning of huge revenue streams for professional athletes in all sports in the 100 or so years of countless celebrity endorsements that have followed.

Today's well-compensated superstar spokesmen and product image-builders, like Michael Jordan, say "Thank you, Albert Spalding."

A Knockout with Trade-Mark Boxing

Packaging is another way that image building EEs have made themselves celebrities and superstars of sorts. One such pair was William and Andrew Smith, makers of Smith Brothers Cough Drops, who—in seeking a means to protect their product—turned a theft deterrent into a selling point through marketing ingenuity.

> Packaging is another way that image building EEs have made themselves celebrities and superstars of sorts.

Finding no other way to prevent companies and apothecaries from counterfeiting their highly desirable (and easily duplicated) product, the brothers Smith decided to distribute only in *pre*-packaged boxes. They figured it was unlikely that small-timers would counterfeit the boxes, as well as the contents—or at least it wouldn't be worthwhile for anyone to try.

The acclaim for these first "factory-filled" packages promoted their popularity, as did the appearance of the word "Trademark," which was broken down into two syllables—TRADE and MARK—and appeared directly under each of the two brothers' likenesses. People started to joke that their first names were Messrs. Trade and Mark Smith.

The packaging was a huge marketing coup, and the brothers' sales shot up a near-vertical curve, with the weight of medicated drops sold daily rising from only five pounds a day to a whopping 8,000—or *four tons* of cough drops out the door every 24 hours—over the brief ten-year span of this phase of their working lives.

All because they became box celebrities with the hack and wheeze world of coughers.

Otis Elevators:
He Made Their Jaws Drop

Gutsy stunts by gregarious extreme entrepreneurs have created self-sustaining lore throughout the saga of business imagery.

As anthropologists and other thinkers illuminate, just beneath the veneer of our "civilized" psyches pulse ancient oral-culture impulses, churning experience and information into mythic paradigms. Whether it's business, sports, entertainment, politics, personal lives, gossip—everything we encounter gets processed. Many of the most colorful moments in our well-documented and greatly mythologized business history have been provided by showboating EEs seeking to make a lasting impression.

> Many of the most colorful moments in our well documented and greatly mythologized business history have been provided by showboating EEs seeking to make a lasting impression.

One celebrated incident occurred in 1854, when Elisha Otis held a public demonstration of his newly designed "safety hoist" elevator at the American Institute Fair in New York City. Until that time, orders for his invention had been very sparse, and the entrepreneur was highly frustrated.

Elevator cables historically were prone to snapping. Otis sought to allay these legitimate concerns by demonstrating how his contraption would halt any free fall if a cable were to snap. So he had himself hoisted in an open-frame elevator far above the mildly attentive crowd and instructed an assistant to slice the cable.

At this, the spectators let out a collective gasp of horror as the car started to plummet—but after a mere instant, the device's safety spring arrested the fall. Elisha proclaimed to the crowd, "All safe, all safe."

While old Elisha Otis died only four years later (of natural causes), his showy legacy lived on. Under his children's charge, Otis Elevators eventually rose to become a thoroughly established industrial force, particularly once steel girder construction ushered in towering skyscrapers.

Where the Image *Is* the Product

In sunny southern California, another extreme entrepreneur has repositioned an entire experience-based product concept, much in the way that Ed Lowe (of Kitty Litter fame) rethought and redirected his powdered clay into an entirely new and fresh concept.

Starting with his awareness of the charming pockets of creativity and legendary communities where free-thinking and artsy-craftsy lifestyles flourish, EE Shaheen Sadeghi set out to harness the essence of Haight-Ashbury, Greenwich Village, and Paris—all under one roof. It was to be an alternative to the sterile, chain-store-filled, muzak-enhanced malls of suburbia.

Thus he created an inspired grouping officially labeled "The Lab," and unofficially dubbed the "anti-mall," in Costa Mesa, California. It was only a stone's throw from the elegant and sprawling, snobby South Coast Plaza of every upscale franchise store known.

Sadeghi's "anti-mall" comprises a group of clothing, candle, and music shops, performance spaces, sidewalk cafés, and an ambient faux post-apocalyptic environment. If you can imagine *A Clockwork Orange* meets the East Village of New York City for a cup of cappuccino (but *not* from Starbucks), you've got it.

Here hipsters can congregate, escape from conformist reality, and strike their revolutionary blows…by spending money…on stuff! Trendy stuff, to be sure. There's also the performance art option, available most evenings at Sadeghi's haunt, whereby street performers can find a comfortable nook or cranny and wail away to the delight of smarter-than-the-average bear (or so they feel) shoppers.

The Lab is obviously a fine example of brilliant marketing, but there's legitimacy to the project beyond its calculated demographic targeting. Visitors are not required to purchase anything, performance spaces are available to a range of inclinations, and Sadeghi encourages people to make creative use of the space.

The Lab isn't a utopia, but it doesn't pretend to be. Rather, it is what might very

> With the more mundane varieties of shopping easily handled online, the bricks-and-mortar universe will have to become more enticing.

well be an early representative of the kind of commercial/social establishment that will flourish as a side-result of e-commerce.

With the more mundane varieties of shopping easily handled online, the bricks-and-mortar universe will have to become more enticing. Some of this is already happening at larger malls, which are shifting into the amusement park mode—such as the world's largest, the Mall of America in Bloomington, Minnesota.

But more edgy alternatives—such as The Lab—are likely to emerge as well. It is also a harbinger of what may lie ahead for many other types of businesses and EEs. Selling image is the commodity of tomorrow.

Taking the Bull (%@*) by the Horns

As we see in business, image is king. To describe consumer behavior, the coin of the entrepreneur's realm is *perception*, and more accurately "perceived value." The impressions that are imprinted or positioned in the mass mind determine buying patterns more than objective criteria do.

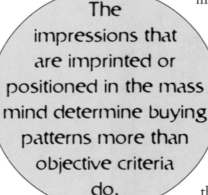
The impressions that are imprinted or positioned in the mass mind determine buying patterns more than objective criteria do.

A common method of trying to manage or manipulate image is what we know now as public relations, which emerged at about the turn of the century to upgrade and "humanize" the image of the corporation. One of the first accounts was John D. Rockefeller, who was trying to repair the image of Standard Oil in the wake of the Colorado coal field killings in which the company and state militia cut down men, women, and children (11 died) in order to break the strike.

The trust-busting spirit was rampant, and in response to the pure disdain that moguls like Rockefeller, J.P. Morgan, and others felt towards "the commoners," Rockefeller was first among them to realize that their heretofore "silence is golden" approach to community relations was no longer adequate. He was the first magnate of lofty and mammoth proportion to humbly and sympathetically reach out to those angry villagers gathering with torches and preparing to storm the gates.

His unexpected openness and feigned warmth caught them off guard, and it worked—quelling what could have been a bloody episode in the chronicle of early American business.

Just *Un*-Do It

On a good day, PR is used to keep a company or a product's image red-apple shiny. On a bad day, it's used to control the spin when a company or product gets a black eye.

Nike's cofounder Phil Knight has a decidedly *un*-nice image. Supposedly the embodiment of the company's "Just Do It" tag phrase, "Swooshbuckler" Knight is a take-no-prisoners kind of entrepreneur. He has built a hyper-macho internal company culture, where employees are encouraged to unleash a lot of high fives and guttural yells.

Early in the 1990s, publicity started to swell about Nike's reliance on third-world sweatshop labor. In shades of Kathy Lee Gifford, and more so than other shoe manufacturers, Nike's high-priced footwear has been produced in factories where awful conditions prevail—including sub-poverty wages, excessive hours, non-permission for bathroom trips, the works.

Despite documentation of the situation, Knight's attitude was dismissive; he made it clear that he didn't care and thought it was all a matter of bleeding hearts. Then a slight wobble in sales helped push the company to give a little and agree to some degree of international inspection. But one of those groundswell movements had already gathered force, with product boycotts and other visible protests taking root all over the country.

The protests haven't flipped Nike's canoe, but they've dealt a blow that no amount of PR triage can fully repair. Ongoing image-building techniques, like the company's heavy reliance on superstar endorsements, certainly stemmed the tide of what might have been a PR disaster and the potential *un*-doing of Knight's "Just Do It." A lesson in it for all of us is how swiftly and decisively image can shift in the public eye.

SUPER SELLING
versus Selling

Nearly anyone who's regarded as being "irresistible" has a natural gift that is perfect for driving sales. Many EEs are certainly imbued with this "follow me" Pied Piper quality. But here is where extreme entrepreneurs and the merely gifted part company.

Sellers simply use the tools of marketing and imagery as props for making a sale and generating revenue. Extreme entrepreneurs are far more intense. They are provocative, aggressive, and seek a connection—and a lasting convert. No matter how long they've been at it, you'll find the EE is *still* selling the dream.

It doesn't, however, require that someone be a born hawker able to sell ice to Eskimos; countless entrepreneurs and even many EEs don't acquire the spark until they encounter a business opportunity that triggers their imagination. Then certainty and passion kick in. Once others see the light and say: "This is a wonderful thing. I believe it makes

8

my world a far better place," the EE's dream, like the proverbial genie, is out of the bottle.

Once someone is interested, a salesman is halfway home. An extreme entrepreneur, however, sees this as mission accomplished—because the rest is simply the irresistible draw of visionary evangelism. It's the *Field of Dreams*, "build it and they will come" concept. And come they do, drawn by the EE's sheer power of complete belief in the idea behind the product, service, or experience. A fervor few salespeople can ever hope to marshall.

As many top VCs allege, better a sparkling visionary EE as the salesperson offering a mediocre product than a mediocre entrepreneur bringing a sparkling visionary product to market.

As many top VCs allege, better a sparkling visionary EE as the salesperson offering a mediocre product than a mediocre entrepreneur bringing a sparkling visionary product to market. Guess which has a better shot at success?

Okay, you get the idea. But not all extreme entrepreneurs owe their triumphs solely to proselytizing. On the strategic side, EE success often rests on an uncanny sense of what will sell and how to sell it. By definition, any entrepreneur who's devised a radical new twist on selling is also an EE through inspired involvement. Such innovations can assume many forms: new types of businesses, modified business structures, updated distribution techniques, or a visionary take on massaging customer relations.

This chapter looks at a varied assortment of extreme entrepreneurs who in some way advanced the process of selling. They are the ones who thought out of the box and left behind a legacy for other EEs to ponder and from which to profit. All were innovative thinkers and actors; and most had charismatic personalities too. The changes they wrought have become permanent moves in the playbooks of all extreme entrepreneurs who follow.

EE Superstar: Richard Warren Sears

Before there was e-commerce, infomercials, and telemarketing, there was the trusty U.S. Mail...and Richard Warren Sears, the extreme entrepreneur briefly noted in Chapter 4 for his historic partnering with watchmaker Alvah Roebuck. However, Sears also made a huge contribution to off-site selling with the legendary Sears Catalog—the grandfatherly precursor to all variations that have since followed—that now also should be noted.

In 1880, 72 percent of America was rural. The true pioneer of the general merchandise catalog targeted at this huge market was Aaron Montgomery Ward. With his brother-in-law, George R. Thorne, Ward sent out first catalogs in 1872. But Richard Warren Sears, who had extraordinary marketing and sales instincts and a thoroughly innovative streak, took this business concept much further.

After getting his start with a consignment of watches, Sears moved to Chicago, expanded his product line, and started fixing watches on the side. With Alvah Curtis Roebuck, he formed Sears, Roebuck & Co. in 1893. Sears also brought a virtual cornucopia of merchandise to the hinterland. By 1887, it sold 24,000 separate items from its 540-page tome of a catalog. To Sears, his true competitors weren't the other catalog operations, but rather local merchants. These merchants fought against the postal changes that made it less expensive to distribute the catalogs, but to no avail.

> Richard Sears also made a huge contribution to off-site selling with the legendary Sears Catalog.

Sears came up with a slew of marketing and selling innovations. Here are but a few:

- Made all Sears catalogs free.
- Employed loads of copy. He had a big flair for composing product descriptions (and advertisements), causing people to buy more because they felt informed about a product.
- Offered scads of special promotions and "freebies."
- Started the first-ever testing lab for patent medicines—later expanded to cover everything testable. If Sears sold it, you could be sure it was good.
- Included detailed product specifications and standards.

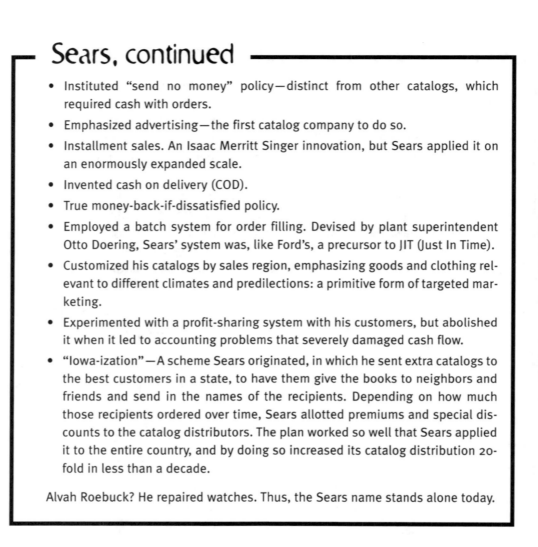

Sears, continued

- Instituted "send no money" policy—distinct from other catalogs, which required cash with orders.
- Emphasized advertising—the first catalog company to do so.
- Installment sales. An Isaac Merritt Singer innovation, but Sears applied it on an enormously expanded scale.
- Invented cash on delivery (COD).
- True money-back-if-dissatisfied policy.
- Employed a batch system for order filling. Devised by plant superintendent Otto Doering, Sears' system was, like Ford's, a precursor to JIT (Just In Time).
- Customized his catalogs by sales region, emphasizing goods and clothing relevant to different climates and predilections: a primitive form of targeted marketing.
- Experimented with a profit-sharing system with his customers, but abolished it when it led to accounting problems that severely damaged cash flow.
- "Iowa-ization"—A scheme Sears originated, in which he sent extra catalogs to the best customers in a state, to have them give the books to neighbors and friends and send in the names of the recipients. Depending on how much those recipients ordered over time, Sears allotted premiums and special discounts to the catalog distributors. The plan worked so well that Sears applied it to the entire country, and by doing so increased its catalog distribution 20-fold in less than a decade.

Alvah Roebuck? He repaired watches. Thus, the Sears name stands alone today.

The Natural

Some EEs *are* born with the persuasive touch, and William Wrigley, Jr. (noted earlier for his premium gum product transition), is the perfect example of a true *natural*.

After many other early adventures, Wrigley settled back near the family hearth for a spell and sold soap for his father before venturing out on his own. He often recounted the tale of his very first customer, a rather timid shopkeeper of sorts whom the teenaged Wrigley cheerfully wheedled all day long and well into the evening. Eventually, the businessman succumbed—after acknowledging that his choices were limited to three: resign himself to accepting the kid as a potentially lifelong companion, kill the lad, or simply buy some soap so he'd go away.

According to Wrigley, the essence of salesmanship is: "Believing in something, and convincing others." But great skill is involved—self-mastery, resilience in the face of abuse, a keen grasp of human nature, enormous effort, and the courage to persist even when everyone else is at variance.

It is a rare salesperson that can adopt the essence of an extreme entrepreneur's vision, but they do exist. It is a wonderful skill that EEs should always be receptive to—for skilled salespeople are few and far between, and are wonderful allies in the pursuit and execution of your dream. For no person—or extreme entrepreneur—is an island.

> It is a rare salesperson that can adopt the essence of an extreme entrepreneur's vision, but they do exist.

Developing a Pick-Up Line

The ultimate prize is to "own a category," a distinction accorded to products such as Jell-O gelatin, Xerox copiers, and Kleenex tissues. Marketing plays its part in the success of such All-Star products, but so does the selling. The Hoover vacuum cleaner is certainly in the league of category killers—especially in England, where "hoover" is considered a verb. And the selling of the thing was at the heart of its success.

Fallen on hard times and employed as a janitor in the Canton, Ohio, area, amateur inventor James Murray Spangler in 1908 invented a lightweight, efficient carpet sweeper to avoid the respiratory distress his employer's unwieldy and ill-mannered behemoth was inducing. In simpler terms, it wrangled the dust problem to tolerable levels.

Selling his patented "electric suction sweeper" door-to-door, Spangler approached his cousin, Susan Hoover, who was married to William "Boss" Hoover, a wealthy saddle merchant. Boss Hoover, who possessed a shrewd EE business mind, clearly foresaw futuristic innovations, such as automobiles and other such revolutionary developments. He also immediately recognized the cleaning machine's looming commercial potential, and promptly purchased the manufacturing rights from Spangler.

> Marketing any new product is always a challenge.

Marketing any new product is always a challenge, but Hoover came up with a masterful plan. He placed a newspaper ad offering a free ten-day in-home trial for the cleaning machines. To the hundreds who replied, Hoover sent a letter telling them that the machine would be delivered through a local business. He then contacted a store in the area and offered the shopkeeper a win-win proposition. If the customer bought the machine, Hoover would pay the store a full commission; if the recipient declined to purchase, the store owner could keep the unit as a free sample. The vast majority of these pleasantly surprised local businesspeople ended up becoming Hoover dealers as well.

Launching the Dust Buster Squad

Even after developing an impressive network of dealers spanning the country, Hoover's sales were not what he'd hoped they'd be. He went out into the field to investigate and quickly realized that the only way to effectively sell such a new category of product was by demonstrating its ability.

Hoover first recruited a small army of door-to-door salesmen and trained them to the hilt. They all had to be able to disassemble and reassemble a machine with flawless military precision, and each received ongoing instruction in sales psychology.

Soon, all across the nation, doorbells rang and housewives marveled as the Hoover dust busters first sprinkled a small bag of debris on the carpets—and then, with a click of a switch, the "beats as it sweeps" magic of a Hoover made it disappear.

Hoover sought to inspire his sales team with an array of motivational publications and novelties—including a company theme song and even their own semiprofessional Hoover baseball team. Creating an avidly enthusiastic, highly motivated sales force—a powerful squad of true believers—and setting them loose with an apt and innovative strategy proved the key to Hoover's success.

Door-to-Store Delivery

Many EEs have had to hoof it at first to get vendors to give their wares a try, let alone offer the goods to customers. As mentioned earlier, Edward Lowe trucked his five pound bags of Kitty Litter from store to store, facing at least as much ridicule as acceptance in the early days.

Another was the founder of the Boston Beer Company, entrepreneur Jim Koch. In 1985 he played a leading role in transforming American beer production—and consumption—through the "micro-brewery-ization" of the nation's drinking establishments.

A top-tier business consultant with a Harvard pedigree, Koch couldn't ignore the pull he felt, imbedded in his soul (as he suspected) by the Koch gene pool of five straight generations of small brewers. Koch experimented until he'd come up with a brew of his own that satisfied his high standards, and he named it *Samuel Adams*. On his first sales call, Koch, who did not consider himself a salesman in any way, approached a Boston bar owner and started to explain what he'd brought. Stammering a bit, and somewhat at a loss for words, Koch finally opened his briefcase, popped a (pre-chilled) bottle and poured a glass for the wary pubmeister, who skeptically drank it down.

> Many EEs have had to hoof it at first to get vendors to give their wares a try, let alone offer the goods to customers.

Closing his case and assuming the worst, young Koch mustered up a weak smile and prepared to turn and leave. The pubmeister growled "not so fast," and immediately ordered 25 cases.

According to Koch, that was the moment of his true birth as an entrepreneur, when he embraced his quest to brew and sell. He celebrated the moment with a cool Samuel Adams himself!

William "Boss" Hoover's success contributed mightily to the mass acceptance of home electrical appliances in general. Eventually, as buying behaviors shifted, the company reverted back to the dealer system as the charm and effectiveness of door-to-door selling began to wane. But not without first taking its rightful place in the extreme entrepreneur's creative selling Hall of Fame.

Conforming to the Big Blue Dream

Thomas Watson, Sr., was the first presiding EE in IBM's history, and was followed by Watson, Jr., another true EE. While Watson, Sr. didn't found it *perse*, the company he was hired to helm in 1914 wasn't yet called IBM—it was C-T-R, a promising but unfocused company that he transformed into the unquestioned titan of tabulation technology and into one of the world's most powerful corporations.

> Much of IBM's formative success is attributed to Watson's emphasis on the sales mission.

Watson considered himself to be, foremost, a salesman—a title he bore with enormous pride. Much of IBM's formative success is attributed to Watson's emphasis on the sales mission. His sales staff was highly trained to heed the customer, to know the product line as well as the engineers do, to radiate enthusiasm each hour of every day, and, above all, to *think* (the ultra-terse slogan IBM once promoted that is still a classic entrepreneurial challenge).

In fact, Watson adopted and then applied many of the techniques he had acquired while working as the general sales manager of the National Cash Register Co., techniques that we tend to think of as Japanese-style business practices. For example, he cultivated and engendered a near-fanatical Kamikaze aura of company spirit and loyalty, with daily songs, family events, and intramural sports teams. He also used sizeable sales incentives to motivate his corps.

Watson exhorted his sales force to emanate excitement, but he required everyone to maintain a consistent, impeccably groomed appearance. This was the birth of the famous blue-suited salesman, the infamous IBM uniform. To Watson, this regimented look expressed drive, professionalism, and somehow progress; but in a later era, of course, this sartorial policy came to symbolize conformism and the old school.

Watson was a perennial preacher of self-improvement and attitude adjustment, long before such advice became a trite commodity. One of his best nuggets was that none of his salespeople should allow their hearts to grow older than 40. "At the age of 40, a person then was older than 72 percent of the country's population—and no one could afford to lose contact with that huge majority if they hoped to make any further meaningful contribution to the world," he artfully noted.

Watson's IBM is a funny, full-circle kind of EE story. Big Blue is legendary, to be sure, and in large part for its distinctive aforementioned sales-oriented strategy. It's a classic American entrepreneurial myth, but one that doesn't always serve as an inspiration to the modern wave of techno-preneurs. IBM has, in fact, come to be known as a sort of stiff grandpaw of a company to the Internet-oriented up-and-comers—your father's Buick, if you will. This tag for one of the trailblazers of technology, the most avant of the avant garde of its time? It's also a warning to entrepreneurial whippersnappers everywhere—today you're the next big thing, tomorrow *you're* the suits.

Studying Selling Techniques

Now no one is going to tell you how to sell your particular dream. But extreme entrepreneurs are like sponges—soaking up small tidbits and scraps of ideas and concepts that are then tucked deep in their bag of tricks. At just the right moment, they are drawn out, carefully assembled, and brought to light in a new and fresh way that often makes the difference– and saves the day.

> Extreme entrepreneurs are like sponges—soaking up small tidbits and scraps of ideas and concepts that are then tucked deep in their bag of tricks.

When Everyone's a Salesperson

Sarah Breedlove (Madame C.J. Walker) was briefly noted in Chapter 5 as an extreme example of shoestring capitalization—starting out with only $1.50 and an amazing "dream." But that was not the chapter to tell *how* she built her successful multi-million dollar hair product empire. Now is the time to add this all-important missing ingredient—here, where super-selling comes in.

In building her hair products mega-world, Madame C.J. Walker devised a new multi-level marketing structure, one optimized and customized for the African-American market. Consequently, her salespeople were earning $5 to $15 a day during a period when white laborers were making around $11 a week.

Mining Firestone Nuggets

Harvey Firestone started his tire company on $20,000, and over 30-something years he built it into a whopping $100 million a year conglomerate. Still, despite all his big city success (in Akron, Ohio), he remained a pea-pickin' country boy at heart—and many of his famous observations still linger on in the business world as home-spun truisms.

> **Firestone was an outspoken sort, and his ideas about selling were typical of his no-holds-barred approach.**

Firestone was an outspoken sort, and his ideas about selling were typical of his no-holds-barred approach. He had no qualms about telling people blunt things that weren't often verbalized or generally heard in most businesses. Firestone noted:

- There are times when the sales force is largely irrelevant to the company's thriving revenues, when the public simply *will not be deterred* from buying.
- Establishing quotas is an unsound practice; it encourages scurrilous deals between salespeople and their clients—as "favors."
- Never buttonhole a sales prospect; never pester. It's not enough to just meet them. In order to start selling, you must arrange or wait for a good time to try to sell. This is common sense.

Indeed. Firestone's homey approach saw him through many achievements—such as inventing the mechanically fastened straight side tire, non-skid treads, low-pressure pneumatic truck and tractor tires, and successfully insulating tire cords against heat build-up. By the mid-1930s, one out of every four tires used in the United States was Firestone.

Starting out with door-to-door sales, Walker soon moved into newspaper advertising, and then she started training women to open up their own hair salons rather than just sell hair products. The more products they sold—and the more additional people they got to sell products themselves—the more inspired and financially rewarded the sales reps became. Sounds an awful lot like the origins of Amazon's modern affiliate program, doesn't it?

Walker's way of training saleswomen emphasized dignity and what would now be called "empowerment." African-American women had never been treated with that kind of positive regard in a business context, and the effect was transformational. The sales and multilevel marketing mechanism was truly revolutionary. Respect—in any form, at any and all levels—is a powerful motivator, never to be overlooked or forgotten. Madame C. J. Walker thought so—and won.

An Army in Pink

Mary Kay Ash's empire has been driven exclusively by sales. Though the multilevel sales system wasn't an Ash invention, she took it to a higher plane than anyone had before.

Her system of "consultants" and "directors" offered many thousands of American entrepreneurial-minded women an instant, dignified avenue into the business world. In Mary Kay's system, a "consultant" who exceeded the sales level necessary to rise to "director"-ship would win a pink Cadillac, which became the symbol of Mary Kay-style sales excellence.

The real returns for any Mary Kay consultant derived from recruiting new consultants, from whose sales the recruiter would get a cut. It became a human conveyor belt delivering a constant flow of new talent into her organzation.

> Mary Kay Ash's empire has been driven exclusively by sales.

Similar in a way to Madame Walker's goals, the central element in Kay's mission was to empower women. But when Mary Kay Cosmetics hit a sales slump in the mid-1970s, Ash realized that the numbers didn't work any longer for most women with ambitions. The average earning was the same as it had been five years earlier—and this was an inflationary period. She decided she needed to boost incentives to attract the same caliber of saleswomen as in the past. When she upgraded the "bonus" structure, sales quickly started to climb again.

In the days ahead, watch as you drive around town and sooner or later you're sure to encounter a pink Cadillac somewhere with a woman at the wheel. It's better than any vanity plate that tips what the driver does for a living. If it's pink, it's Mary Kay—because she *owns* this clever idea. And the driver is one of Mary Kay's legion of devoted, motivated—and successful—sales reps. Or else it's Bruce Springsteen, though you'll probably be able to tell the difference.

One Word: Plastics

Mary Kay Ash trained her sales force to go out and conduct two-hour beauty-tip seminars and product demos, but face-to-face in-home interactive marketing was the brainchild of Yankee extreme entrepreneur Earl Tupper.

Not only did Tupper devise a major product innovation with his airtight, temperature-resistant line of food storage containers, but he also invented a similarly innovative sales technique: the classic *Tupperware party*.

After trying to sell his goods through stores yielded tepid results, Tupper came up with the idea of holding parties all over America, generally hosted by a housewife who would invite friends, relatives, and acquaintances to see—and buy—the line of wares. The hostess would then receive a gift for her troubles: naturally, a gift of Tupperware. What a surprise!

Not to be ignored, astute EEs like Madame C.J. Walker, Mary Kay Ash, and Earl Tupper reached out and drew others into their dream—in such a way that it built a wonderful universe of small dreams for thousands of mini-EEs within their sphere of influence and under the gentle guidance of the principal visionary.

Bricks or Clicks?

The new frontier of e-commerce has spawned profound innovations in the selling and buying processes.

Jay Walker's priceline.com, for instance, has turned the terms of traditional commerce on its head, armed with nothing much more than a very strong, smart sense that consumers were ready to use the Internet to take control of the buy/sell process. Walker proposed that consumers could "name their price" for products or services such as airline tickets, hotel rooms, and cars, and motivated sellers could meet that price, with priceline.com acting as a clearinghouse/facilitator/matchmaker between consumer and seller. This unique type of e-commerce, known as a *demand collection system*, enables consumers to use the Internet to save money on a variety of products and services and sellers to generate incremental revenue without disrupting their existing distribution channels or retail pricing structures.

Using a simple, irresistible selling proposition—name your price—priceline.com collects consumer demand (in the form of customer offers guaranteed by credit card) and matches it to supply (through a network of participating sellers and their databases). The priceline.com model works for the customer, he or she names a price on an item and never has to feel victimized by prices that are out of his or her control or ability to pay. It also works for the sellers: priceline.com manages an ever-changing list of acceptable prices from potential sellers, and if the customers bid at or above the seller's offer, the deal is on. If not, there's no deal for the moment, and the customer is encouraged to keep trying. Consumers feel as if they're getting the chance to haggle; companies feel they're retaining ultimate control. Think *The Price Is Right* meets eBay.

> The new frontier of e-commerce has spawned profound innovations in the selling and buying processes.

This isn't just some technological innovation; it flies in the face of a whole bunch of conventional wisdom about selling. For instance, it assumes a buyer is willing to commit to a transaction without knowing the brand of product he or she may end up with—so much for the oceans of dollars spent by companies in the last half-century to develop brand loyalty, eh? And it assumes a buyer is willing to be flexible in order to get the price he or she is looking for. In the case of airline tickets, the buyer signs up to buy a ticket without knowing when the flight might take off. It also assumes a level of trust that somehow only the Internet has nudged out of the consumer; the buyer has to commit a credit card for an instant sale if the offer is accepted.

It's clear Walker studied what we're all learning about the consumer's willingness to experiment in the Internet commerce hothouse (eBay, Schwab Online, etc.) and found his opportunity to reinvent commerce as we know it. With the help of a clever, quirky little marketing strategy involving the highly recognizable, but utterly out-of-place actor William Shatner, he's convinced more than seven million registered users to help him revolutionize the marketplace; priceline.com facilitates the sale of more than 15,000 airplane tickets daily, and has sold more than five million in less than three years in business. That's a lotta sales.

The Gang Is Here

Another new buying/selling paradigm is being offered by a handful of e-commerce sites in the form of what is known as *online aggregate buying*. The idea behind aggregate buying is that consumers can gather together, or *herd*, and commit to purchasing a certain item on the promise of the substantial discount they can earn buying as a group.

Founded by Tom Van Horn on as entrepreneurial challenge posed by Internet pioneer Paul Allen, the now-defunct Mercata.com facilitated aggregate buying through its patented technology and innovative model. Mercata offered consumers what they call "Power Buys," limited-time buying periods in which product price drops as more shoppers sign up to participate in the buy. So a person might register for a buy, allowing a willingness to pay, say $500 for an item, and by the time the buying period has ended 24 hours later, the price may have ended up at $200, thanks to the collective purchasing power generated by many participants.

Mercata is gone, but the idea lives on. While the idea of group buying and co-op buying is hundreds of years old, this contemporary twist is pure extreme. It operates as the online opposite of an auction; in an auction, the more who participate, the higher the price goes. In an aggregate buying model, people work together to drive prices down, powered by the speed and mass-ability of the Internet. In Mercata's case, hundreds of products were offered and its strategic relationships with more than 150 manufacturers and distributors of popular consumer products allowed for products to ship directly from the manufacturers or distributors, leaving Mercata hands-free on warehousing and distribution.

The World's Lowest Prices

Scot Blum is an extreme hotdog who, in 1998, barged into the world of Internet commerce and took aim at none other than Amazon.com. Using a selling proposition based on price alone, and promising no less than "the world's lowest prices," his buy.com rang up $120 million in revenue in his first year in business—the fastest launch in American business history.

Blum operates on the premise that customers for anything will never again be so cheap to acquire. And relying on eyeball economics, he believes that by aggregating many millions of consumer or would-be consumer eyeballs to his sight, his real estate and audience becomes extremely valuable to advertisers desperate to get their product in the increasingly electronic face of the consumer. In effect, his goal is to become the premium online advertising venue, the Super Bowl, if you will, of the Internet.

Blum admits his business model is a thoroughly modern hybrid of selling goods and aggregating eyeballs. By offering "mind-blowing selection," "fast and efficient shopping" (according to *Computer Shopper* magazine), informative online order tracking, killer customer support, and a price-matching pledge, he seems to be collecting more than eyeballs. Acknowledged as the largest technology e-tailer and the undisputed low-price leader, buy.com offers its three million customers nearly a million products, and has been named by *Forbes* a "Best of the Web" retailer for the second year in a row.

> Blum's goal is to become the premium online advertising venue of the Internet.

When the "new technology sector" finishes its feverish dance on Wall Street, sites and businesses like priceline.com and buy.com, like many other extreme Internet start-ups, may not even exist. But their twisting, tweaking, and reinventing of selling has steered commerce onto a new road forever.

Everyone's a Home Boy

Back on terra firma, Hawaii, businesses thrive on the bustling tourist trade and set prices high for the one-shot in-and-out *haoles* (visitors/mainlanders). But to garner and maintain repeat local customers, these same businesses are quick to knock off a cool 20 to 30 percent if you are a *kamaaina* (local).

This goes for stores, hotels, airlines, many island visitor sites, parks, and attractions too. Hawaiian merchants continue *kamaaina* pricing because locals are long-term, repeat customers. If you're going to be there a while, these merchants want your business. And they let you know it in a way that really counts.

So it goes between the *kamaainas* and merchants of the islands, and it is a practice worthy of note for the extreme mainlanders. Do you treat your customers like tourists or locals? Devise your own new traditions and develop extreme ways to let them know you care, and that you want their business forever.

Perhaps the most extreme lesson on selling is that it all comes back to the vital basics lost or forgotten in the ultra-modern hustle and bustle— personal attention in an impersonal world. The Internet has on the one hand made it possible to reach billions; on the other, it's made it more important that your prospect not feel he's been spammed, but that he's been sold to on a one-to-one basis.

RUSTLING UP THE RANCH HANDS
Extreme Hiring

n a fledgling enterprise, every hiring decision has an impact on the company's destiny. At minimum, any new addition to a small staff will influence the quality of daily work life. The selection of, say, a director of marketing or a CFO can be a make-or-break move. Not only do top-level managers need to be skilled or gifted in their respective fields, but they must be able to harmonize with the entrepreneur's style and vision. A start-up with an excellent team of professionals but a somewhat flawed business plan is more likely to prevail than one with a rock-solid product but an inharmonious staff. To apply a biological metaphor, in staffing up the entrepreneur is assembling the organism's genes—the x and the y factor, as it were. This is an especially tricky task during the phase when unknowns still predominate.

An extreme entrepreneur's distinct vision can more than fill a room sometimes, and it can be exceedingly difficult to hire and delegate. And yet, often strategic hiring is the key to the entrepreneur's ability to realize his or her dream—the idea exists, but what is really

9

chapter

needed are the partners and soldiers who can help take it all the way. Unfortunately, there's more than a little "If I want it done right, I'll do it myself" in the entrepreneurial air. So for the EE, the main hurdle might be in first acknowledging the need for a management team.

One classic example is Thomas Alva Edison. Among the greatest inventors of the modern era, Edison proved unable to attain business success even vaguely commensurate with his innovative genius, mainly because he couldn't manage—or hire someone else to manage—his way out of a paper bag. Edison ran his venture like a captain with a crew of deckhands but no officers. He wasn't skilled at financial matters either, and the manager he did hire to cover that base, Samuel Insull, wasn't much better. So all-star innovator that he was—and catalyst and icon of American history— Edison was a bit of a dud as an entrepreneur.

Fair warning to the would-be entrepreneur: If you can't turn a great big huge lightbulb of an idea like, well, the light bulb in to a successful venture, you're missing some of the pieces of the board game.

Hire Away

Even the most renegade extreme entrepreneur—if he or she is smart—knows you can't do it all, so immediately the smart EE looks to fill the gaps. The goal (at the start anyway) isn't to become some mainstream corporate mega-employer of hundreds. The goal is to bring in just the people necessary to execute the vision. So the EE who's an idea person brings in a crackerjack manager or CFO to help make it happen. Knowing what you need (in other words, knowing what you *can't* do) is the key to extreme hiring.

> Even the most rene- gade extreme entrepreneur knows you can't do it all.

Bill Gross of idealab! is just such an extreme entrepreneur. A virtual dynamo, he can barely keep up with his own good ideas. The 40ish Californian was already several entrepreneurial experiences deep into his career when he founded idealab!, a venture that births, incubates, and funds a whole range of online businesses, including eToys, jobs.com, tickets.com, and NetZero, to name just a few. According to Gross himself, his previous experience taught him his

Flaming the Fans

In an Olympic Games program, Home Depot has hired 116 Olympics athletes to work in its stores, walking the aisles as advisors. The point is to boost the company's own employees' morale—not a nontrivial issue for a corporation that employs over 210,000 people. The presence of the athletes is meant to provide a kick to workers, help recruit new ones, and perhaps offer an example of disciplined achievement.

This is nice, in theory, but with company plans to increase payroll by more than 100 percent in upcoming years, maybe Home Depot better be addressing the very high rate of employee turnover it has developed recently. Home Depot has long attracted skilled employees through an aggressive and generous benefits program and an environment that encourages and enables employees to advance to positions of greater responsibility and authority. Somewhere along the way, though, founders Bernie Marcus and Arthur Blanks have lost the hard-charging enthusiasm of their orange-aproned workforce. A Web site tartly named <homedepotsucks.com> chronicles ecological insensitivity, nonsensical waste, and an atmosphere not always positive for women and minorities as the primary complaints. As many a company has discovered, disgruntled employees, in big enough numbers, can put the skids on even the most successful extreme endeavor faster than you can say two-by-four.

strengths and his limitations. As he told *BusinessWeek*: "I don't like managing the details when a company is up and running." Once he figured that out, he began handing over the reigns of his baby businesses to savvy managers like his brother Larry, who's got a particular gift for executing Bill's big ideas.

It Takes One to Know One

Perhaps this generation's all-time, all-star examples of hiring in the extreme are Yahoo!'s CEO Tim Koogle, eBay's CFO Meg Whitman, and Cisco Systems' John Chambers. Each of these strategic hires helped to take the extreme entrepreneur's vision to the next level and beyond. Take a look.

Tim Koogle was Yahoo!'s sixth employee and may even be its oldest—he's nearly 50 years old, in a company where the average age is 29. Yahoo! founders Jerry Yang and Dave Filo knew just what they were looking for in a chief helmsman for the company: a smart, experienced tactician with the heart of an entrepreneur. Indeed, Koogle's business savvy has been critical to the growth and success of the company; he brings balance and the benefit of his experience as an entrepreneur, engineer, and executive to a lively entrepreneurial environment. He's been called the voice of reason, the seasoned veteran, and the cool head. He's a pragmatic consensus builder, decisive and focused, and has taught Yahoo! a thing or two on its way to its nearly $10 billion valuation. Many believe Koogle's being the grownup in a room full of somewhat undisciplined creatives and techheads has made all the difference.

Meg Whitman has been an equally strategic hire for Pierre Omidyar's trailblazing online auction mecca, eBay. A veteran of management stints at Hasbro and Disney, Meg Whitman has described her job as President and CEO of eBay as "helping an army of entrepreneurs to build the world's largest online personal trading marketplace." This would explain why Whitman is considered so important to the success of eBay; she sees herself leading the hundreds of thousands of member/entrepreneurs of the eBay community, and when she helps them, she helps eBay. Known for her sharp brand and consumer instincts, Whitman has worked side by side with Omidyar to forge eBay's powerful community-commerce business model.

Through some notorious periods of technological growing pains, Whitman has kept eBay focused on the consumer, all the while masterminding the company's expansion into premium product auctions and global markets. Unlike many other Internet "celebrity-companies," Whitman's managed to see that eBay, which now has a $20 billion market valuation, has not expanded beyond its reach. As Whitman puts it, "This company was bootstrapped, and we spend money like it's our own." Just the kind of employee you want minding the till.

> Unlike many other Internet "celebrity-companies," Whitman's managed to see that eBay has not expanded beyond its reach.

Technically, John Chambers is just an employee of Cisco Systems, the world's largest networking equipment developer. Cisco was founded in 1984 by Len Bosack and Sandra Lerner, the Stanford techhead entrepreneurs who mortgaged their house, maxed out their credit cards, and finally (fatefully) took a $2.5 million investment from VC Don Valentine to launch their dream. Pushed out by Valentine and the management team he brought in to grow Cisco, Bosack and Lerner cashed out and left Cisco to the suits in 1990 (more on the Cisco story in Chapter 12). Some would argue this is lucky for Cisco stockholders—when Chambers took over the helm of Cisco in 1995, it had $70 million in annual revenues, 300 employees, and a market cap of $600 million; today, it has $18 billion in revenue, employs 31,000 people, and has a market cap in the neighborhood of $500 billion.

What makes Chambers such a superhero? Cisco wanted to become the IBM of networking and Chambers has made it happen. He brought progressive management and unmistakable leadership to a company poised on the brink at a critical moment in the history of technology. Through fanatical emphasis on customer service, and on leveraging his empowered, communicative workforce, Chambers has radically expanded Cisco's capabilities. Chambers is one of the top executives in the world, and though his experience never overlapped with the founders of Cisco Systems, his entrepreneurial zeal has turned the company into an Internet powerhouse that stands shoulder to shoulder with Microsoft, Intel, and even GE as one of the world's most valuable companies. When asked who her hero is, aforementioned Meg Whitman answers "John Chambers." It takes one to know one.

You Gotta Believe

According to many reports, Amazon.com's hiring requirements include an all-out commitment to the company's mission—despite the fact that the company is a bit young to be said to *have* much of a mission beyond survival and growth. It has been said Amazon seeks to hire "people who want to care—people who want things to do that matter—people who want a life with meaning, who want a career with meaning." In turn, Amazon rewards this wholehearted commitment by providing employees "...with a voice and a responsibility for their actions." If that sounds like a campaign speech, well perhaps Amazon is campaigning to be the biggest store in the world. (The company's inspirational motto of "Work Hard, Have Fun, and Make History" is probably not as big on brotherhood as "'So help me Sam," but Amazon did happen to lasso a few top-ranked execs from Wal-Mart along the way.)

The Body Shop's Anita Roddick has spoken about her frustrations in finding people who can instill her stores with the verve and excitement she believes they stand for. "If I had to name a driving force in my life, I'd pick passion every time," she said. This is something that's not taught in business school, as she well knows.

The Body Shop for many years eschewed advertising, instead relying on good word-of-mouth. Roddick has always aimed to educate customers. So her workers must be able to smoothly articulate ideas and information. Her solution is to tap the energy of "the anarchists" to keep a company vibrant. Such anarchists generally aren't found amongst the ranks of managers and executives, she says. And Roddick doesn't believe in hiring people with the intention of molding them into what you seek. If you want passion, then look for passion and hire passion, she believes.

This Town Isn't Big Enough

For some extreme entrepreneurs, hiring other entrepreneurially inclined people is fraught with controversy. Some companies, such as 3M, try to cultivate that quality in all its workers, so it seeks out this entrepreneurial spirit, unafraid of the possibility that these workers will fly the coop. Other business owners say it's the worst idea of all to hire people with established entrepreneurial traits, because they'll just use company resources until they have enough of their own to make another go. One thing seems certain: *Autocratic* EEs are better off *not* hiring other entrepreneurial types or renegades. The entrepreneurial nature is too independent for this dynamic to pan out in the long run.

> For some extreme entrepreneurs, hiring other entrepreneurially inclined people is fraught with controversy.

Former California Governor Jerry Brown is an extreme entrepreneur trapped in the body of a politician. Bright, innovative, controversial, fearless—Brown cheesed off more than a few people in his years as head of the Golden State. One of the favorite ongoing dramas of his tenure was his problematic relationship with his Lieutenant Governer, Mike Curb. Curb, an engaging, clever guy in his own right, was an odd-couplish Republican match to Brown's woolly Democrat. Their union was strained, competitive, even combative. So much so that Governor Brown got to a point where he avoided leaving the state because Curb loved to step into the leadership void when Brown was gone and make executive decisions of his own in his boss's absence. Now this was politics, and there was no board of directors to break up the scuffling, but it was a perfect example of two strong-minded visionaries for whom one could argue there just wasn't room enough.

The Fine Art of Profiling

The mix of industry segment and a given company's lifecycle stage determines the profile of the ideal hire. For example, during Intel's "adolescence," the company needed a very special blend of traits in the managers it hired. As CEO Andy Grove described it, they realized the company was essentially "a manufacturer of high-technology jelly beans." On one side of the spectrum, brilliant young technical visionaries generally would be unable to ensure that the jelly bean assembly line kept running at peak efficiency. On the other side, however, production-oriented types lack the scientific skills to contribute to the ongoing creation of new and improved jelly beans. So the company sought gifted professionals with their feet on the ground—technical specialists who take well to working within a highly structured framework. This, of course, is a rare breed.

> The mix of industry segment and a given company's lifecycle stage determines the profile of the ideal hire.

To gather the kinds of management teams it needed, Intel applied several strategems. The owners tried to blend seasoned professionals and relatively inexperienced engineers, to strike a balance of mutual influence. They also ran a very aggressive college search program. Once they had staffed up, they used a market-based organizational model (where work teams of specialists operate independently, but within a unifying framework) to deploy their engineering talent. But they chose a very different framework for their manufacturing operations, employing a modular approach akin to a franchise model (where teams operate as separate, independent entities).

It's a Free Agent Nation

The world of work is undergoing a tectonic shift, and I don't mean casual Friday. I'm talking about the fact that more than 25 million Americans currently work as independent professionals. They're nearly 25 percent of the working population and their number is growing at an explosive rate.

This workforce is morphing in part because corporate loyalty (from both sides) ain't what it used to be, but mainly because the economy has changed, business and industry have changed, and right now, the expert individuals with the skills to solve a problem rule.

> More than 25 million Americans currently Work as independent professionals.

How does this help the extreme entrepreneur? The extreme entrepreneur can think of this free agent nation as a great big pool of highly skilled knowledge workers, primed and ready to help ramp up operations, or fill in gaps on a project-by-project basis (say, parsing out individual PR efforts, or MIS) as the venture grows. These independent professionals are happy to have traded in a company time card for the freedom and flexibility their workstyle affords. An EE would be wise to develop a corps of outside specialists to come in on a project-by-project basis, leveraging the outside expertise without bringing more to the burgeoning infrastructure.

Check out smart sites like <www.Guru.com>, which matches "gigs," as they call the indivudual pieces of work-for-hire, with "gurus," the specialists who can do the job. As evidence of the explosive growth in this sector of the workforce (also known as the "Talent Market"), Guru had put more than 200,000 free agents together with more than 20,000 hiring companies—before they'd even clocked a year in business.

Intel's "signing bonus" incentive was relatively attractive during the 1970s: about $10,000 worth of Intel stock, with the option of participating in Intel's company-wide stock-purchase plan. With time, and especially with the advent of the Net, Intel has had to boost its perks and salaries greatly, but it still can't compete with the prospect of retirement at 25. Suitable Intel managers are those for whom the cachet of working for the world's pre-eminent chip firm—the *gourmet* jelly bean factory—exerts a special pull.

Long before today's acute shortfall of skilled technicians and executives in Silicon Valley, the competition among employers was fierce. So when Intel was building a new wafer-processing facility in Livermore, California it started to hire workers several months before operations ramped up, bussing them 35 miles, twice a day, to train them at the Santa Clara plant. Intel developed this farm league approach that enabled the hiring and honing of the splendid mix of specialists that have made the company great.

Guns for Hire

The last ten years have demonstrated that Human Resources—especially in the area of executive level hiring—aren't always able to keep up with explosive entrepreneurial growth. In other words, there aren't always enough good managers around to fill the critical roles in the extreme entrepreneur's start-ups. The problem is that no matter how well-positioned to break out, a start-up often has trouble attracting the all-star talent already enjoying corporate tenure in Fortune 500 land. Who knows how many yearlings have floundered due to a dearth of leadership? What's an extreme entrepreneur to do?

> The last ten years have demonstrated that Human Resources—especially in the area of executive level hiring—aren't always able to keep up with explosive entrepreneurial growth.

One solution is to let the people with the biggest stake in your success help you staff your operation. Virtually all venture capital outfits are actively matching their start-ups with strategic hires, the managers and marketers and finance types that can take the entrepreneur's good idea all the way to the Winner's Circle. When this sort of staffing can make the difference between the premature death of a start-up and its ultimate success, you can see why the VCs are pulling strings to give their ventures a leg up.

All the fancy venture firms insist on aggressively participating in the hiring process for their companies, from Kleiner Perkins Caufield & Beyers to Matrix to Morgan Stanley. And Bill Gross's idealab! incubator/venture outfit is entirely built around this infrastructure-in-a-box idea.

Sometimes the venture firms even have to announce that the party's over, as Flatiron Partners did when they nudged Kozmo.com founders Joseph Park and Yang Kong off the top rungs of their "last-mile" delivery service. As a principal backer of the innovative start-up, Flatiron knew when it was time to bring in the grownup to run the show. Now CEO Gerry Burdow calls the shots, leaving visionary founders Park and Kong free to drum up deals and publicity—and to raise more capital, of course.

Another solution is to take advantage of all the free agents out there and bring in the specialists on a contract basis. Hiring contract executives allows even the greenest of start-ups to take advantage of the immeasurable experience of the seasoned veterans. There are lots of appealing reasons a contract executive might sign on to fill the void, including the challenge of an entrepreneurial endeavor without the personal risk, as well as a high level of flexibility and freedom.

> Hiring contract executives allows even the greenest of start-ups to take advantage of the immeasurable experience of the seasoned veterans.

One thoroughly modern way to fill the staffing gaps is to make the potential hires offers they can't refuse—give 'em equity! You've heard all the stories of the unlikely dot.com millionaires, the early A-teams who took company stock options instead of industry level pay and are now living la vida loca on some island in the Caribbean. Giving executives and employees equity in the form of shares or options provides them with a very real stake they can hang their hats on—for the long haul.

In spite of Microsoft's myriad problems with Uncle Sam, its employees have stuck to the company like glue. Year after year, companies like Amazon.com and Sun Microsystems furtively send outside recruiters to make a pass at Microsoft smarties. They wait until Microsoft's semi-annual stock option vesting date, then swoop in and try to lure away a willing few. So far, though, there have not been many takers, mainly because of the loyalty bred of sharing the wealth and value of the company. And the promise of more.

It's a Team Thing

Ask any extreme entrepreneur who's succeeded with a venture and he or she will tell you that beyond initial survival concerns, growth and team-building are the next—and most difficult—challenges. You can staff up all you want, using any or none of the above-mentioned strategies, but if you can't actually hand off the baton, you're never going to get beyond the everyday stuff that stands between you, growth, and profit.

> Ask any extreme entrepreneur who's succeeded with a venture and he or she will tell you that beyond initial survival concerns, growth and team-building are the next—and most difficult—challenges.

Extreme entrepreneur and marketing maven Seth Godin has been through every stage and grade of teambuilding. In the years between the germ of an idea for Yoyodyne, his Internet promotions and marketing firm, and its ultimate purchase five years later by Yahoo!, he went from working alone in his underwear on the third floor of his old Victorian house to helming a young, creative staff of more than 40 people. Godin was attracted to people like himself—smart, nimble, driven. He hired them as fast as he could find them.

As the company grew and the stakes got higher, it became clear that Yoyodyne's original flat organization—an admittedly appealing part of its corporate culture—could not support the growing pains of this free-wheeling gang. Bright and energetic, his young staff needed old-school management—supervisors, executives, the whole shebang. In Internet time, there wasn't the luxury of building a company and culture brick by brick the way, say, IBM did. Godin scrambled to pull a squad together, using recruiters, his own board of directors and investors, and even friends as invaluable resources. Once there was an infrastructure—and team—in place, Godin, an idea man and torchbearer extraordinaire, was free to go out and beat the drums for his venture, rather than spending undue time teaching new workers how to work.

So even though it's tempting for the extreme entrepreneur to try to go it alone—even in an officeful of people—it's critical to transcend that tendency and bring in the specialists. No entrepreneur is an island, after all, and hiring is a vital part of building a bridge to success.

MANAGEMENT
Magic

Throughout business history, nothing has been more thoroughly studied, reviewed, and continually revised than the subject of management. Many trends have come and gone, such as decentralized management in the form of *quality circles* from Japan, European *task force teams,* and Scandinavian's socialistic *unisystems*. There have been new hybrid management systems emerge called *simulated decentralization*, which somewhat diffused pure true management with quasi-worker bee involvement. Most of these techniques were employed with limited success, lackluster response, negligible results, and extremely short lifespans.

Maybe these techniques and strategies—as enlightened as they seemed at the time—failed because management isn't a system you can prescribe and administer. Management is leadership, plain and simple, and good, effective leadership doesn't come from management principles or techniques, it comes from people. All the strategies and tactics examined by students of management are no more than the

chapter

tools used by a leader to execute goals. The true leader (and effective manager) is a maestro, using every instrument at his or her disposal to make the magic happen.

What's to Manage?

The easiest way to break down the components of a company—that is, *what* needs to be managed—is to look to Tom Peters' and Robert Waterman's seminal *In Search of Excellence*, in which they sketched out the framework of a company. The seven elements of this framework—*strategy, structure, systems, style, staff, skills,* and *shared values*—are, in the simplest terms, the pieces of the picture of any company.

> The seven pieces that comprise the frame-work of a company are strategy, structure, systems, style, staff, skills, and shared values.

In a perfect world, the strategy and structure of a company would support the system, staff, and skills that constitute its infrastructure, and reflect a style and shared values unique to the company (corporate culture, in new millenial-speak). These eight balls are what the leader/manager would hold in the air in somewhat perfect balance, in this ideal world. Ha! A company with a staff of two is likely to be able to focus on only a couple of these elements at a time, and that's on a good day. How can a big company with 30,000 employees pull it off?

The fact is, they do. And the difference between success and failure at it is often measured in the extreme.

Like I Said, What's to Manage?

The seven hungry monsters of the framework described above vie desperately for your entrepreneurial attention, every minute of every day you're in business. But the true variables, the elements that really make up the challenge of being an entrepreneur, are what separate the extreme from the, well, ordinary. Growth. Change. Pursuing long-term goals while battling daily challenges. These are the mountains the entrepreneur must climb, whether alone or supported by a cast of thousands. The extreme entrepreneur certainly has the most distinctive approach to the climb.

Personality Counts

One of the most common characteristics of the EE's approach to management is the cult of personality. Many of the most extreme and successful entrepreneurs in the history of doing business have taken their personal appeal and leveraged it into an entire business—systems, infrastructure, culture, the whole shebang. The looming personalities of these entrepreneurs are often second in importance only to the business products themselves—and even that is not always so. At Southwest Airlines, for example, it's impossible to tease apart the selling proposition from Herb Kelleher's ultra-personable management style.

> One of the most common characteristics of the EE's approach to management is the cult of personality

Indeed, Kelleher's very aware of his critical role as torchbearer in the success of Southwest Airlines. But why peddle the personality? Because he knows his fun-loving, zany pranks reputation is more than just a happy face on the company's supreme leader—his employees are attracted to, identify with, and perpetuate his signature good nature. Under his distinctive leadership, Southwest has become the most consistently profitable, productive, and cost-efficient carrier in the airline industry. It has also earned the industry's coveted "Triple Crown" for best on-time performance, baggage handling, and customer satisfaction for four years running.

To Kelleher, the goal has been to build a "culture of commitment," spending less time on traditional management efforts such as benchmarking best practices, and more time building a company that values the "human touch" as much as quality and dependability. This has been the key to Southwest's ability to deal with change in a volatile, competitive industry. Kelleher and Southwest employees know exactly who they are, and in the face of change, this doesn't change. As Kelleher himself has put it, "Life is chaotic; in the airline business it's anarchic. So rather than trying to predict what we'll do, we try to define who we are and what we want....we reflect, observe, debate—and we don't use our calculators."

Growth is another of the mountains Kelleher has tackled alongside his employees. Acknowledging that managing a multi-billion dollar company is different from managing a million dollar company, Kelleher says, "Change your practices, not your principles" as you grow. As his own company grew beyond the reach of his personal attention, he figured out ways to communicate with the large number of people under his umbrella, using videotapes, newsletters, weekly updates, and frequent, memorable visits to the field. This way, Kelleher asserts, your people are as aware as you are of what's going on in the company, in the industry, and in the marketplace. Then they're personally inspired to "buy into a concept, to share a feeling and an attitude, to identify with the company—and then to execute."

> Herb Kelleher of Southwest Airlines says, "Change your practices, not your principles" as you grow.

Another result of growth and the way his role changed was an inevitable shift toward delegation. As Kelleher put it, "You delegate more and more, and make yourself available as a troubleshooter....And you remember that systems are not masters—they are servants in helping you carry out your mission. Nothing comes ahead of your people."

Insurance industry iconoclast Bob MacDonald has a similar organic relationship with his employees at LifeUSA. His ownership model has cultivated plenty of *esprit de corps* among the worker bees, who are highly motivated by their personal stake in the collective effort. They are equally motivated by their feelings for MacDonald. As Maggie Hughes, LifeUSA's COO, has described MacDonald, "He's very disciplined and gives very clear directions on what the expectations are. He has a tremendous ego, but it's in the right place; he's very grounded. And he's very witty and likes to have fun." LifeUSA employees are keen on the way their boss flouts business conventions; one day, he brought a marching band into the office to boost morale.

MacDonald himself describes this as a way of managing, engaging in shenanigans that help break down the barrier between people, especially employees and management. His team appreciates that he doesn't stand for most of the traditional standards on how business should be conducted. They're proud to be identified with him, as the renegades of the insurance industry.

Steel Bonds

Nucor Steel's Ken Iverson knows well the power of the force of personality. He has used it to revolutionize his industry, flip the traditional management paradigm on its head, and blaze new trails in employee relations. For starters, he took Nucor, a failing conglomerate, from the verge of bankruptcy, restructured it around its few steel operations, and then galvanized the steel industry by introducing the use of mini-mills to make steel, instead of the old huge vessels. Mini-mills are much more efficient than their predecessors, and now produce half the steel made in the United States.

> Nucor Steel's Ken Iverson knows well the power of the force of personality; he has used it to turn his industry upside down.

Iverson's also notorious for decentralizing the company's management structure—there are barely 20 people in its corporate offices. The rest of the responsibility falls on the shoulders of the people closest to the operations themselves—the ones, according to Iverson, who are in the best position to make decisions.

In pursuing his goals, Iverson even reinvented the management of information; he established an innovative, scaled-back internal reporting method, in which performance at the multibillion-dollar company can be essentially summarized in several pages of meaningful statistics. The result of this "Cliff Notes" approach to internal reporting is a drastic reduction in redundant data manipulation, unnecessary meetings, incompatible messages among managers, and superfluous effort. He encourages employees to report to him on an informal basis, a quality for which he is famous. Iverson said once to *Worth* magazine, "A basic principle is that anyone in the company—any employee from any plant—can call me or the president

EE Superstar: Jack Stack

Extreme entrepreneur Jack Stack is the patron saint of employee empowerment. Stack is CEO and president of the Springfield Remanufacturing Corporation, a rebuilder of engines and engine components in Springfield, Missouri. He started out at SRC's former parent company International Harvester as a mailboy. He hustled and learned and worked his way up to become plant manager of Harvester's remanufacturing plant in Springfield. When Harvester hit a rough patch in the early '80s and had to sell off assets, Stack and 12 other managers bought the Springfield plant to save it from bankruptcy.

Stack was a plant manager, not a CEO, and was admittedly unsuited for a traditional corporate role. Nor did the company have the luxury of cultivating a traditional infrastructure. Stack himself has said, "We didn't have time to write mission statements or value statements. Our mission statement was simple: Don't run out of cash."

> **SRC's workers were trained to be able to understand the most minute detail on a balance sheet, the problems were identified and attacked.**

Stack had to lower operating costs quickly, and the fastest way he could think of to find the places to make cuts was to let the entire workforce see where the company was on paper and enlist their help in strategizing. So SRC's workers were trained to be able to understand the most minute detail on a balance sheet, the problems were identified and attacked, and SRC went on to grow from 119 employees to more than 650 employees, and from $16 million in sales to almost $70 million in the first ten years of operation.

From this seat-of-the-pants problem-solving came Stack's now celebrated Open Book Management strategy, which he believes works because it creates an environment where people are empowered and motivated to succeed. In giving employees ownership, plenty of open communication, and total involvement in business planning, he unleashes a mega-motivated employee base.

From the start, Jack Stack exhibited an acute awareness of the direct impact his business decisions might have on his employees' lives, and his employees have returned the favor over and over again.

or the general manager at any time. That's why we generally answer our own phones."

He's got the charisma, too, to get the troops behind him. He's accessible, he's visible, he's innovative in the way he takes care of his people. He's proudest of Nucor's policy of giving every employee a sizable annual stipend for four years of college for each child. His employees appreciate that financial support, as well as the message it sends their children, that education is important and worth contributing to.

Like a lot of those high-wattage personality type managers, Iverson's held in the highest regard by his people, but also given wide berth by them when things aren't so hunky-dory. For instance, when a machine at Nucor breaks down, the team assigned to it doesn't get paid until it's fixed. It's the price you pay for allegiance to this variety of extreme entrepreneur.

Mount Minor

Halsey Minor, C|Net's founder and chief executive, isn't a textbook-perfect, *Entrepreneur Knows Best* kind of guy either. His intensity often turns volatile, and his employees accept the fact that Minor can be a major bear. He's known for micromanaging, for example, pestering project managers over every tidbit of minutiae. When C|Net's Web master was trying to ready the site for launching, he eventually had to put a sign on the door asking that Minor stop looking at the site.

Until 1997, C|Net actually had no formal employee-evaluation or budgeting processes in place, which meant a perpetual chaos of seat-of-the-pant decisions. Further, Minor is known for his hot/cold interactional style, either lavishing someone with profuse praise or blasting them with volleys of 6 A.M. incendiary e-mails.

There's also a huge upside to Minor's managerial ways. C|Net has always been a cool, let's-do-it, freestyling environment, young in all ways, including spirit. Minor may be unpredictable at times, but he's a stone visionary who's held the company together through some very rocky patches. C|Net is akin to the CNN of the wired world, and its EE reflects that level of monumental aspiration.

> C|Net is akin to the CNN of the wired world, and its EE reflects that level of momentous aspiration.

When Tough Love Is Just Plain Tough

Sometimes management by personality really boils down to management by fear. Citigroup's Sanford Weill may be the king of this particular scenario. A dealmaker of the most extreme kind, Weill's first venture was a tiny private Wall Street brokerage, which, through a brilliant, 40-year string of strategic partnerships and acquisitions, became Citigroup, the world's biggest financial firm, comprised of securities, banking, and insurance concerns. It is said he is a perfectionist, driven to be the "master of every piece in the puzzle."

> Sometimes management by personality really boils down to management by fear.

His success is built on a complicated tapestry of deals and acquisitions. Weill made these maneuvers work by forcing employees to focus on teamwork. He'd remind his employees, "The enemy is the guy down the street, not the one in the next office." He encouraged cross-division support, and developed a sort of enforced loyalty by rewarding managers with stock, which they were forbidden to sell.

He gets right in the thick of every level of corporate activity, grilling employees, intimidating them, paralyzing them with demands, "managing by gossip." He also involves himself in the personal lives of his employees, attending weddings, funerals, even bar mitzvahs; there are so many mixed feelings about their amazing, high-profile boss, his employees don't know which end is up. Love may not be what they feel, and loyalty might not quite describe it either, but a stomach-churning fear could come closest to how Citigroup's 190,000-plus employees feel about their supreme leader.

Horse Sense Management

Occasionally an entrepreneur shows his or her extreme colors by fearlessly following the path of values-driven common sense. Ellen Gordon, president of Tootsie Roll Industries, comes from a long line of such entrepreneurs. Her family has controlled Tootsie Roll for more than 65 years. Her grandfather sold paper to the original company and noticed that it was late paying its bills. Her grandmother smelled an opportunity and saved up a little of her teacher's pay to buy up Tootsie Roll stock. She encouraged other relatives to do the same, and before long (and thanks in part to the Depression) the family had amassed a controlling interest in the company.

Ellen grew up in the candy business, and after college, she and her husband took over the company, committed to staying on par with their rivals in the fiercely competitive candy business by embracing new technology. Gordon invested in high-speed machines and solicited valuable employee feedback, which enabled them to move forcefully forward into the modern chocolate age.

She still solicits employee feedback. Says Gordon, "As a manager, you really don't know all the answers," and people at every level feel free to share their points of view at meetings. This culture of common sense has created a work environment that few care to abandon; the company doesn't track turnover because most of its employees have been there for more than 20 years.

All this homespun lore shouldn't be taken to suggest that Tootsie Roll is some friendly, sleepy company-next-door. It may not be as big as the Candy Kings, Hershey and Mars, but it's one of the largest, and controls a solid, strategic portion of the candy market. Recent acquisitions of brands such as Junior Mints, Mason Dots, Sugar Daddy, Charleston Chew, and Charms Blow Pop have enabled Tootsie Roll to shore up against potential takeovers. Gordon is committed to keeping Tootsie on top and independent, and intends to leave behind a company her family or employees can run.

In spite of Tootsie Roll's impressive history of earnings and dividend increases, Wall Street doesn't pay much attention to the publicly-traded company. Ellen Gordon is quite tight-lipped about the company, in part to keep any sale or takeover speculation at bay. And she makes no apology; Gordon has said, "We're busy making Tootsie Rolls. We haven't spent a great deal of time with the investment community. And why should we? It would only call attention to our business, and we're not interested in that."

Just Run It

When an entrepreneurial endeavor takes off right out of the gate, there's not a lot of time to ponder management issues—you just do it. DEC's Ken Olsen remembers his own early challenges as a start-up artist inventing the technology that was his core business at the same time he was figuring out how to manage those people innovating alongside him. He describes one of the greatest tasks as getting people to feel that whatever they are doing is their invention.

Says Olsen, "Developing and managing an organization like Digital was a compromise or a set of paradoxes...conflicts between leadership and giving responsibility to others. It's obvious that the leader [me] can never be expert in everything. We have to be dependent on those people who are. They have to have the motivation that comes from them setting the goals. And yet we have to have a common goal, and that is the job of the leader."

Sew Simple

If ever there was a Zen management style, women's clothing designer Eileen Fisher would be its spokesmodel. She is low-key, as are her minimalist clothing designs, but make no mistake—she's an extreme entrepreneur of the first order. The volatile, often vicious fashion industry still scratches its collective head at her phenomenal success, mainly because every bit of her entrepreneurial story goes against the conventional grain. She started with no capital (okay, it was 350 bucks), no Merrill Lynch-type backing, no slick publicity. She just showed up at a trade show one year with a handful of designs and went home with $3,000 in orders. The second show brought her $40,000 in orders, the third $90,000. It has been just such an exponential explosion ever since.

> If ever there was a Zen management style, women's clothing designer Eileen Fisher would be its spokesmodel.

Everything about her business defies fashion industry logic. She shuns Seventh Avenue for a funky Hudson River-front warehouse 45 minutes from New York City. She doesn't worry about what's happening from season to season in Milan and Paris and New York; she just goes about her business serving up classics to her avid working-woman clientele. Heck, she doesn't even know how to sew!

Fisher manages her 300-person company with the same common sense reflected in her clothing designs. Her gift is in surrounding herself with smart people with whom she feels a natural trust. Her workplace ethic is very organic, very simple: "Our work environment should be comfortable, just like the clothes. This is our life and we want to enjoy where we work." The tenets of her management technique are equally simple: Engage people's creativity. Team with people. Empower people. Look at the big picture. Create a joyful atmosphere. Tell the truth. Keep it simple. Be yourself. Know yourself. Know your people.

Eileen Fisher runs her company the way she runs her life. She credits her success—multi-million dollar company, 20-plus Eileen Fisher shops, with nearly 1,000 stores carrying her clothes nationwide—with her ability to relate to her employees and especially to relate to her customers…because she is her own customer.

To the Trenches!

Sometimes the extreme entrepreneur motivates and manages a workforce by generating a follow-me-into-the-trenches loyalty, a sort of boot camp approach to getting the job done. This is certainly true of iVillage CEO Candice Carpenter, who admits she doesn't have time to nudge people along in a traditional time frame. Her company and her industry are developing too fast, so she uses an approach she calls "radical mentoring" to get people moving along faster than they would in a normal corporate environment.

Carpenter, who got her own leadership training as an Outward Bound instructor and working under entertainment execu-preneur Barry Diller, doesn't suffer thin-skinned, slowpokes lightly. She believes that if you aggressively urge your people to self-mastery, they can get past the need to prove themselves and on to creating value. She uses radical mentoring to rush her people into the fulfilling role of creator. Think of the way a drill instructor teaches the mastery of basic skills, all the while chiseling away at the recruit's ego. In other words, she's consciously growing leaders, not followers, and she's using edgy, extreme ways of doing it.

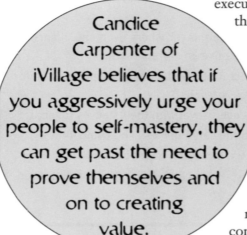

Candice Carpenter of iVillage believes that if you aggressively urge your people to self-mastery, they can get past the need to prove themselves and on to creating value.

Carpenter's aware that her prospects must sign up for this approach, or else it'll just feel like abuse to them. She acknowledges that this sort of accelerated growth hurts, that the prospect has to accept the terms of this approach, and that Carpenter herself has to be 100 percent committed to the person she's mentoring. Carpenter says to her prospects, "I would like to move you along faster; are you game?" Because if the person doesn't consciously submit to her methodology, no one succeeds and everyone's unhappy. Willingness is key.

She works through stages, first getting her employees to stop thinking of themselves, then to remove pride from the work equation, next to wean them from praise, and finally to focus on creating and serving. Carpenter has described her own goal as creating a culture where work is its own reward, instead of winning praise from higher up. In short, it's about the work, not the person. When the employee achieves this level of consciousness and creativity, Carpenter has herself a new leader.

Dead serious about this truly radical approach to managing her company's 200 employees, Carpenter has hired only five senior level staffers from outside; the rest are homegrown.

Did Someone Say War?

Sometimes entrepreneurs who rely on trench-loyalty are truly dragging the whole company with them into all-out war. Take Tom Siebel of Siebel Systems and Larry Ellison of Oracle. Siebel went to work for Ellison in 1984, during the early years of Oracle, and was named the company's top salesperson worldwide for selling 280 percent of his quota (this in his first year on the job). Siebel was no wallflower himself, but he learned plenty from his flamboyant boss.

By 1991, Siebel was on his own and started Siebel Systems, a technology company based on a marketing information system he developed in his days at Oracle. He started his company, which specializes in software used to support sales forces, with his own money (no VCs, no investment firms) in a dilapidated warehouse in East Palo Alto, California. A decade later, Siebel Systems is a $3 billion dollar-plus business with 68 percent market share.

> Sometimes entrepreneurs who rely on trench-loyalty are truly dragging the whole company with them into all-out war.

One of the keys to Siebel's extraordinary success is his ability to sell—to potential customers, partners, even his own employees. Until 1995, most of his people worked for stock. When his company went public in 1996, Siebel had a personal net worth of $280 million, but more importantly, he had turned 40 of the 150 loyalists working for him into millionaires—the company is 70 percent employee-owned. It has been said his people are driven by *his* drive.

Siebel himself told *BusinessWeek*, "We're trying to build a world-class company—an Intel, a Hewlett-Packard, a Xerox, a Charles Schwab—a company where we achieve unprecedented levels of company satisfaction, where we're recognized as a clear market leader. A company that's recognized globally as a great place to work." All that, and a company that tweaks the mustache of Larry Ellison every single day.

Get to O.R., Stat!

Microsoft has an unusual way of managing teams during the intense period toward the end of a product development cycle. Kathleen Hebert, general manager of Microsoft's project-management software business invented the "triage meeting" to battle the "bug," those glitches and hitches that plague the process and product when each new iteration of the software is released. Six or so functional managers meet seven nights a week in the last two months of a development cycle to ruthlessly prioritize, eliminate obstacles, and set immediate action items in front of their people.

As Hebert told *Fast Company*, in triage, "Issues are decided in a very unambiguous way and quickly communicated to the team." This high-octane decision making can't be maintained on a full-time basis, but it does allow for priorities to become clear in the immediate. Said Hebert, "We bring in all perspectives—technological, business, customer—and constantly ask ourselves, 'Is this the hill we want to die on?' The trade-offs immediately become clear. Triage is about the immediate conversion of decisions into action. It enables us to deal with tons of issues at a feverish pace—without sacrificing quality."

Actually, Siebel Systems was in no way a competitor of Oracle—Siebel made customer relationship management (CRM) software while Oracle dominated the database software category. Nonetheless, Ellison certainly saw Siebel Systems as a challenge and his former protégé as a competitor. So in 1999, Ellison launched his own CRM line, devoting 900 programmers and hundreds of millions of dollars to wedge himself into this category that falls outside of his core business.

The two men are known by friend and foe as fearless, arrogant, brilliant businessmen equally bent on winning, and especially bent on beating each other. Both are charismatic, tightly wound, winner-take-all types who demand employees be as committed to winning as they are. Says former Oracle president Gary Kennedy, "Tom is the best blend of someone who has extremely strong technical skills, sales skills, and business building skills. It is rare to find all three. Tom would hate for me to say this, but the only other person I know who has that unique combination of skills is Larry." *That* explains a lot.

The existence of the landing lights and control towers of management systems, and the support staff to implement it, doesn't always protect a

Extreme Entrepreneur

174

strong-willed entrepreneur from himself or herself. In many cases, as noted above, the strong will and distinctive personality of the entrepreneur overrides systems and infrastructures and all the other company components we outlined at the outset of this chapter. That's not to say those elements don't come along for the wild ride, but it's always very, very clear who's driving the car.

Extreme Hall of Fame

Perhaps the best modern example of management as leadership is mega-extreme entrepreneur Jim Clark, most famous for founding Netscape, with Marc Andreeson. Clark has been described as the most successful serial entrepreneur of our time, the only entrepreneur to have personally launched three separate billion dollar companies: Silicon Graphics, Netscape, and Healtheon/WebMD.

> Perhaps the best modern example of management as leadership is mega-extreme entrepreneur Jim Clark, most famous for founding Netscape, with Marc Andreeson.

Born in rough Texas country, Clark was a high-school dropout who stumbled onto his aptitude for mathematics after a stint in the Navy. He went on to get a fistful of degrees, and invented a computer chip that enabled inexpensive 3-D modeling for engineers and provided the foundation for his first successful venture, Silicon Graphics.

After spending 13 years painstakingly building SG, Clark walked away with a measley $16 million, a fact he blames on the venture capitalists he was forced to bring in to fund his cash-strapped company in the early years. Clark had to trade shares and control to keep his firm afloat, and in the end was squeezed out by a mercenary CEO who saw Clark, the visionary, as an obstacle to the organization.

He went on to found Netscape with Marc Andreesen and a group of young University of Illinois smartypants, and one sale to America Online (AOL) equals $2 billion of personal profit later. Clark was immediately on to his next entrepreneurial adventures, including Healtheon and an online photo developing company called Shutterfly.

Clark has distinct ideas about what it takes to lead, especially as an entrepreneur. He has said that leadership "comes from a combination of being persuasive; believing in what you're doing; having integrity...and knowing how to judge good people, because you can't afford to have anything but good people early on in a company." Clark says he looks for intelligence and humility in his people, and collaborators who know how to listen and take advantage of what others have to offer.

He attributes his success to a deep restlessness and an ability to attract and sustain the attraction of good people. Even though he's had some of the best billion-dollar ideas of the last century, Clark believes the idea is not as important as the people.

Clark told *Context* magazine, "There is no real way to tell whether an idea is good until you have people thinking about it, working on it, and proving it. If really good people get enthusiastic about what seems like a good idea, it makes them more likely to be successful. A leader must strive to get the very, very best people—people who threaten you because they're smarter than you. You also have to make sure you don't have high turnover. I have a rule: Never lose the first good person."

THE PERILOUS
Journey

The entrepreneurial endeavor on the smallest scale is by nature risky, an adventure not everyone is cut out for. Even the most conservative, least daredevily entrepreneur is sticking his or her neck out there—three out of five new entrepreneurial ventures fail within five years. That's more than enough risk, especially for the average Schmoe.

The extreme entrepreneur, however, attains the spectacular—on a grand, global, mega-profit scale, on a wow-what-a-great-idea scale, and especially on a massive crash-and-burn scale. This chapter concerns itself with the occasional crash-and-burn part of the extreme experience—the dangerous moments on the way to becoming a revolutionary as well as the moments that sometimes represent the fatal end. Now by end, this might mean the first of many ends, as the EE is well known for that phoenix-rising-from-the-ashes quality. The EE is nothing if not resilient and persistent, and so what looks like the bitter end is often just the signal of a new beginning.

This chapter will describe several train wreck stories, as well as some bounce-back tales. What you'll learn is that the road to extreme entrepreneurship is dangerous—even treacherous. But you'll also see that some of these perils are familiar and identifiable, and therefore somewhat avoidable if you keep your eyes open.

Basic Business Blunders

Some incredible innovators, such as Thomas Edison, didn't kick down doors as entrepreneurs, and thus they're the extreme entrepreneurs with the asterisks next to their names, the ones who just don't make the final cut. Edison, as an example, lacked a critical component or two required of the truly extreme entrepreneur. Edison had no ability to gauge his own strengths and weaknesses, and accommodate for the latter.

> Thomas Edison, as an example, lacked a critical component or two required of the truly extreme entrepreneur.

Edison wasn't just some wild-eyed scientist with no head for business. He fully understood that creating companies for the manufacture and sale of his inventions would be critical. He also knew enough to realize he needed help in pulling that off. But the people he chose to execute the building of a business around his innovations were not suited to the challenge.

He once said, during this period, "Hell, there are no rules here—we're trying to accomplish something!" A healthy dose of rules and decent management might have enabled Edison to profit as he should have from the huge amount of wealth generated by his breakthrough.

In 1892, just four years after forming Edison General Electric to support the commercial development of his inventions, he sold his interests in the company to the group that would ultimately be known as commercial and industrial giant GE.

Edison went on to obtain 1,093 patents for his inventions, the most by any individual. He bounced back enough to form Thomas Edison Inc. years later and certainly didn't die a penniless man. But in the end, he wasn't able to take his brilliant ideas and turn them into the thriving, legendary businesses they deserved to be. This would be in the category of crying shames.

Auto-Matic Errors

There are those who succeed brilliantly on some level and then fail flamboyantly in a repeating cycle—EEs with flawed judgment or self-sabotaging behaviors, but EEs nonetheless. The definitive Exhibit A for this category is the father of General Motors, William C. Durant, whose name has been eclipsed over the decades by Henry Ford and Alfred Sloan. Durant had vision and exuberance to spare, but no commensurate grasp of cash management.

> There are those who succeed brilliantly on some level and then fail flamboyantly in a repeating cycle—EEs with flawed judgment or self-sabotaging behaviors, but EEs nonetheless.

Durant wasn't one of those automotive titans who got his start at the engineering table or with his head under the hood of some vehicle. He was an organizer, an empire builder, and knew how to leverage what other people were inventing and doing to forge his entrepreneurial vision. His first such gesture was to buy the patent rights to a two-wheeled cart for $50, then organize the Durant-Dort Carriage Company, which became the largest maker of horse-drawn carriages in the country. Then he founded the mighty General Motors Corporation on the stooped back of the struggling Buick Motor Company, only to have it taken away from him by banking entities who forced him off his own board due to his financial recklessness.

After his first ouster, he went out and started Chevrolet with Louis Chevrolet, who didn't take long to leave the company that bore his name because he couldn't bear the rash way Durant operated. Durant then used his big profits from the hugely successful Chevrolet models to buy up GM stock and regain control of the company. This return to the throne was temporary, though, as he was forced out once again. Next he founded Durant Motors and attempted to create another conglomerate, but ultimately failed.

This entrepreneurial trajectory is exhausting to observe, but you just don't feel sorry for the guy. He didn't mind his money, didn't learn his lessons, and behaved like a serial entrepreneur in the worst possible sense of the term.

What *Was* He Thinking?

Then there are times when the extreme entrepreneur has everything going smoothly, but ultimately doesn't embrace the central market reality. DEC founder Ken Olsen is a prime example of such a cautionary tale.

> Then there are times when the extreme entrepreneur has everything going smoothly, but ultimately doesn't embrace the central market reality.

Make no mistake; as the granddaddy of the modern computer industry, Ken Olsen is a true hero. After World War II, he and his scientist buddies from the Navy and Massachusetts Institute of Technology developed the first fast, relatively inexpensive mainframe-type computer, finally breaking down the price and technology barriers that were keeping the vast developments in electronics and computing from revolutionizing business and industry.

Olsen was prohibited from calling this groundbreaking product a computer, because the federal government (the customer he was looking to land at the time) had announced a moratorium on purchasing computers until every computer it had already purchased was understood and in full use. So Olsen called it a Programmed Data Processor (PDP), circumvented the government's restriction, and delivered them the machines they were looking for to begin collecting seismographic information.

Olsen and DEC went on to develop smaller, faster, more flexible minicomputers for a wider and wider range of commercial use, paving the way for the personal computer revolution of the 1980s and beyond. Some might say that Olsen missed his big chance by not realizing in the early '70s that soon it would be easy for just about anyone to make personal computers. Olsen and DEC made a conscious decision to stay the course

Classic Pitfalls

Over his half-century career, business and social analyst Peter Drucker has consistently presented the business world with canny insights. After decades of observing business behaviors and outcomes, Drucker distilled the four typical mistakes that undo entrepreneurs at new and growing businesses. All of them, he says, are foreseeable and avoidable.

1. *Knowing better than the market.* The entrepreneur fails to contend with the fact that their new product or service is succeeding elsewhere than their target market. In essence, the entrepreneur rejects unexpected, unplanned success because it rattles their belief that they're in control.

2. *Focusing on profits.* Cash flow is the real name of the game, because growth-spurt companies need continual stoking with fresh money. Drucker says an entrepreneur should start planning the next round of financing *six months before* crunch time. Of course, few do—a failing that Drucker attributes to financial illiteracy among most business people, not just fledgling entrepreneurs.

3. *The management crisis.* After about four years of normal, healthy expansion, a company usually outgrows its management base. The entrepreneur has gotten stretched to the max, and when things start to go haywire—as they invariably will—no one is available to take up the slack. Again, acting *before* a crisis is key. Twelve to 18 months before this bottleneck, the entrepreneur should gather those workers who show managerial promise and assign suitable roles. Then there's enough time for them to learn their specialties, for the team to coalesce, and for the owner to identify and replace any wrong choices.

4. *Loss of perspective.* Once the company is up and running, a different type of danger looms. Focusing on his or her desires or needs, the entrepreneur neglects to make the needs of *the business* the highest priority. An entrepreneur needs to be honest in determining whether they have the skills or strengths the company needs at that time. If not, then it's best to step aside or adjust one's role.

with the company's original focus on networked, interactive computing. Even though DEC certainly had the technology and the experience that no other firm had, and was therefore, one might argue, perfectly poised to bust the personal computing biz wide open, Olsen respectfully declined.

Olsen recounted years later, "The goal we set about when we started the company was to introduce interactive computing. And we did that with the first PDP-1. "We concentrated on [integration and networking] because the PC, as it was being developed, was so easy there'd be many people making it," Olsen said. Generally we avoided it and [instead concentrated] on the problem of networking them but not planning to be the large producer of PCs. We formally decided that was not what we were going to do....The IBM success in that business was, for a number of reasons, partly happenstance, partly luck, but to a large degree because they had the size, the resources, and the experience to set up the infrastructure to deliver millions of computers. It was not a matter of invention, it was a matter of management and resources. They were the ones who could do it. After they had done it, it became easier for others to enter the market. Their contribution was good, competent management. And we were off doing other things."

Off doing other things? While IBM et al carved up the personal computer market and laughed all the way to the bank, no doubt. Ken Olsen is the giant they're talking about when they refer to the shoulders of giants. But while his decision not to go PC was thoughtful and purposeful, it surely goes down in history as a classic shoulda-coulda-woulda.

> Ken Olsen is the giant they're talking about when they refer to the shoulders of giants.

Don't Look Now

Ron Stegall is the kind of entrepreneur investors, among others, love to hitch their star to. When he decided to launch LiL Things, a chain of baby mega-stores, in 1993, he had a whole crowd of well-wishing people egging him on and handing him money. His concept was strong: build 30,000 square-foot stores, fill them with the widest possible variety of upper-end children's merchandise (furniture, toys, clothing, diapers, safety products, even food), keep the prices competitive, and provide a friendly, stimulating environment for kids. The stores featured extra wide aisles to accommodate families, a photo studio, a hair salon, even a play area called LiL Land where kids could try out toys. LiL Things was to be a distinctive, one-stop shop aimed at developing loyalty in a powerful customer category—parents with infants and small children.

Stegall's background was strong: he'd been a key executive with Tandy Corporation during its explosive, early growth years, and he'd founded BizMart, an office-supply superstore chain of 57 stores that ended up being acquired by Office Max. His primary investors, Donald Phillips and CeCe Smith, were a couple of seasoned venture capitalists with a great track record with retail start-ups like PetSmart, CompUSA, and The Sports Authority. Stegall had no trouble raising the $28 million he needed to begin to roll out stores nationwide. The idea was sound, the EE was smart, and the money was there. What could go wrong?

Talk about not being aware of the market reality. While LiL Things was busy building a brand and a chain by the book, its fiercest competitor, Baby Superstore, was dogging its every step, unbeknownst to Ron Stegall and company. The first day LiL Things opened its doors, Baby Superstores started turning up right next to LiL Things shops and offering much better prices to boot. Baby Superstore founder Jack Tate, a wacky, wily entrepreneur, made forcing the end of LiL Things his mission, and it didn't take much to muddy up the market and make it an immediate battle to the death. When Toys 'R Us bought Baby Superstore in 1996, LiL Things investors made a mad dash for the exits, and by 1997, LiL Things was bust, after burning through roughly $53 million of investors' dollars. Ouch.

Flatline

Who thought stately, white-haired 70-something Surgeon General C. Everett Koop would turn extreme entrepreneur when he finished his stint as Surgeon General in 1989? In 1997 the man brilliantly leveraged his high-value high profile as the nation's doctor into a snazzy little Internet start-up called drkoop.com, which he formed with a small team of investors.

The consumer-focused interactive Web site was created to provide consumers with comprehensive healthcare information, as well as access to medical databases, health-related publications, medical news, and the ability to purchase healthcare-related products and services online. Sounds like the prospect for a decent consumer experience, as well as an opportunity for lots of interested Internet and medical field parties to partner up and exchange favors. With an $88.5 million IPO in June of 1999, drkoop.com's stock ran as high as $45 in its first year as a publicly traded company.

Rhyming Reasons

The adage "history repeats itself" is obviously meant to be taken figuratively. Despite similarities among people, places, and conditions, the interplay of particulars in any given situation in time is distinct. As Mark Twain supposedly quipped, "History doesn't repeat itself, but sometimes it rhymes."

In broad terms, most EE failures happen time and time again, have loads in common, and can be attributed to one or more of the following reasons:

- Inability to handle rapid growth
- Unsustainable financial requirements—in other words, chronic cash flow crisis
- Misguided acquisitions
- Lack of a flexible management team, representing diverse competencies
- Once-inspirational entrepreneurial style becomes overbearing
- Choice of wrong successor (most common in family businesses)
- Vision obscured by innovation—the product is king and we are its humble servants
- Inability to relinquish reins or delegate to appropriate degree—in a word, micromanaging

Unfortunately, while Dr. Koop and company may be able to take their own temperatures, they're not so good at mapping the path of an expensive start-up. Drkoop.com ended up on life support, due to: (1) an out-of-control burn rate (they plowed through $50+ million in the six months after IPO, but they brought in a meager $9.4 million in revenue for the whole year); (2) a massively underachieving advertising-revenue based business model (even as the second most frequently visited site among the nearly 17,000 health sites on the Internet, drkoop.com didn't come close to winning the fierce battle for advertising dollars in this category); and (3) a dearth of that cash-rich strategic partnering everyone was banking on. To top it off, add a nasty little class action lawsuit by shareholders who allege that the company concealed information regarding the viability of drkoop.com, and shares of the company dropped to a low of under a dollar.

Just three years after inception, Dr. Koop himself became a nearly silent, mere 7 percent owner of the company that bears his name, and "vulture" capitalists took control of 20 percent of the company's value as well as the day-to-day management and long-term planning at a bargain basement price of 35 cents a share. This is not so much the fault, perhaps, of the good doctor himself, as it is of the unprecedented shakeout in Internet land caused by frenetic competition, cash-ravenous dotcoms, and sharkish VCs driving the process during good times and bad. Perilous indeed.

Get Back on the Horse

One true test of an entrepreneur's mettle, of course, is an ability to cope with failure—and to use it as a source of business wisdom. For some, a business foundering is a traumatic trial by fire, while for others it's just the way that cookie crumbled. Among the EEs who rebounded from early business flops feeling stronger and wiser is Anita Roddick.

Founder of the Body Shop, Anita Roddick says she and her husband couldn't handle the first business they established, a restaurant. Also running the inn housing the eatery, they were exhausted by the grueling pace of the work. What saved them from feeling defeated, she claims, was a willingness to admit the mistake and move on.

> One true test of an entrepreneur's mettle, of course, is an ability to cope with failure—and to use it as a source of business wisdom.

Necessity— invention's ultra-fertile matriarch—helped out too, as Anita's husband felt impelled to take a multi-thousand mile outdoor journey, leaving her for a year or so with the charge of supporting herself and their children. She couldn't get by on her teacher's salary alone, so the wheels started turning and she decided to open a natural, environmentally-conscious cosmetics store on a $6,500 loan. Today there are over 1,500 shops in 47 countries and Roddick is world renowned as an entrepreneur and an activist.

Sometimes You Stumble

Even with Anita Roddick's remarkable success, there was a moment when the Body Shop's trajectory threatened to take an unpleasant dive. By the early '90s, her outspoken political activism had reached a critical mass and suddenly she was known as a political figure rather than an entrepreneurial one. This shift in perception caused a backlash, especially in Britain, and when she sensed the business was stagnating (or worse), Roddick took a sharp turn back toward the mainstream, at least from a management perspective.

She hired professional managers to shift the focus of the business full scale back to the business itself. They also built, albeit retroactively, some infrastructure that enabled the now large and sometimes unwieldy enterprise to function efficiently and react to changing markets and competition. She hasn't stopped acting like an activist; she's just brought some smart outside strategies to her unique, innovative approach.

Next!

In fact, for numerous EEs, the first business (or businesses!) is merely a test run—a hurdle they take in stride, and move on past, skinned knees and all. For example, Steve Case launched Quantum Computer Services—which later morphed into AOL—from the embers of the failed Control Video Corporation, a mere footnote now.

> For numerous EEs, the first business (or businesses!) is merely a test run—a hurdle they take in stride.

P.T. Barnum, showman and extremely extreme entrepreneur, had more than his share of stumbles, though it's unlikely he would ever have identified them as such. Arguably the most famous man of the 19th century, Barnum knew everyone of note of his time, from presidents and queens to celebrities and inventors. An entrepreneur right down to his bones, he'd started out as a youth selling lottery tickets and ran a newspaper. He invented beauty contests and baby contests, and made millions in real estate, which he lost when several large fires wiped him out, and then lost again on some bad investments.

He bounced back with a vengeance and created a larger fortune even than the first with his ultimate success, "The Greatest Show on Earth," before his death at the age of 80 in 1891. You might think of Barnum as "just a showman," but he was an extreme entrepreneur extraordinaire and

Give It Another Spin

Many EEs are known for their second or even third go-through, the first ones—the flops—providing the crucial lessons that allowed them to triumph with the next. Walt Disney's first venture ended in bankruptcy, for example, and R.H. Macy, H.J. Heinz, and George Westinghouse failed the first time through. Some, like Heinz, were actually sued for fraud, as was Fred Smith. These are EEs that aren't easily discouraged.

One especially clearcut example was Berry Gordy. Gordy blew it by refusing to give the people what they wanted in his first venture, a record store. He was a jazzhead, and looked down on the blues as a primitive form in comparison to the complexity, virtuosity, and scope of jazz. Of course, he was right about jazz, just as he was wrong about the blues. His refusal to stock the music his immediate market craved wasn't merely churlish; it was just plain dumb. But Gordy was a fast study and his next project (once he convinced his sister to risk some more of the family's limited capital on his venture) became one of the world's great record companies—Motown Records.

> Many EEs are known for their second or even third go-through, the first ones—the flops—providing the crucial lessons that allowed them to triumph with the next.

taught the world a thing or two about succeeding as an entrepreneur. Said Barnum: "Engage in one kind of business only, and stick to it faithfully until you succeed, or until you conclude to abandon it. A constant hammering on one nail will generally drive it home at last, so that it can be clinched."

Premature Evacuation

Some EEs suffer the "failure" of selling their stakes too early or for too little. When the companies they founded and nurtured go on to attain immense valuation, these EEs are left understandably bitter at their own blunder. Warren Avis divested his car rental business in 1954, for a mere few million dollars. Had he held on to the company for another decade—or even kept a portion of ownership—his bounty could have been multi-fold more. Self-sabotaged by his own restless EE spirit, Avis remained regretful over his decision to cash out the business he'd conceived and raised.

Regretful is a polite way of describing how a founding EE feels when he or she gets out before the baby goes platinum. When Cisco Systems founders Sandra Lerner and Len Bosack accepted VC firm Sequoia Partner's infusion of cash at a critical moment in the growth of their company, they traded away ultimate control of the business—a critical mistake. Sequoia brought money, management, and a management process to the venture, none of which had been there up to that point. Before long, Lerner and Bosack's quirky techno-centric approach got in the way of the imported management team, who demanded, as a group, that either Lerner leave or they would. When Lerner left, so did Bosack, and the two almost immediately sold their two-thirds share of the company for $170 million. Sure, we'd be angry at being given the heave-ho by a group of management stiffs, but would we sell our two-thirds share just to wash our hands of the whole thing? Well, knowing that Cisco's worth hundreds of *billions* now, the answer would be, unequivocably, no.

> Regretful is a polite way of describing how a founding EE feels when he or she gets out before the baby goes platinum.

After Halsey Minor "bombed" with his childhood triple-decker-checkers scheme, he went on in college to develop a fairly avant computerized apartment-finding service that foundered when he graduated. He then launched mega-successful C|Net, so no big loss to the naked eye, but Minor regrets having abandoned projects such as his apartment-finding service. With the wealth of such services abounding on the Web right now, you can see why he's a little wistful.

Extreme Hall of Shame

When it comes to the perils of being an extreme entrepreneur, there are few stories as extraordinary as John Z. De Lorean's. A meteor shower of an EE during his time, De Lorean's name has become a code word for a certain kind of danger in the business world.

De Lorean was a gifted engineer, corporate manager, and charismatic visionary who shot up the ranks at GM, apparently destined to become the corporation's youngest-ever chairman. But serious friction between De Lorean and the top brass at GM led to his dismissal. De Lorean claimed the conflict was based on his perceptions that the marketing and money men were failing miserably in producing good cars. Others said his outsized ego bridled at operating within the strictures of a large organization. For whatever reason, in 1974 De Lorean set out to become the first successful new entrepreneur in the car business since Walter Chrysler in 1925. His plan was to design, build, and market a unique, luxury vehicle.

Trading on his stellar reputation as one of the most irresistible sales personalities in history, De Lorean cobbled together an astonishing blend of private and public monies to finance his extremely high-risk project. The logistics involved were enormously complex, involving hundreds of parts manufacturers as well as the building of a modern assembly plant in an economically blighted district of Belfast, Ireland. His drawing board depiction of the DMC-12 was magnificent, and the look and idea of the machine were a key driving force. To add to De Lorean's astronomical exposure, he knew that to make the company fly he would have to roll out a winner on the first go, sell 18,000 to 20,000 cars right off the line to establish a base level of profitability, and *then* go public with a huge equity offering to finance expansion and diversification.

The near-inevitable snafus with technology, production, and supplier arrangements started to pile up almost immediately, dictating that De Lorean's projected $15,000 jet-set buggy would have a $26,000 price tag instead, eroding its prospective market with each upward price-point ratchet. Needing more funding at every step meant De Lorean had to engage in extreme brinkmanship with the British government—even as it underwent a changing of the guard during the car's development. An implicit part of the "deal" was that the government was to look good by facilitating the creation of 2,500 good jobs for the beleaguered Northern Irish—and by splitting the slots evenly among Catholics and Protestants. Nevertheless, as bad press about the "American con man" began to overshadow the good, British leaders began to balk at additional cash infusions.

Despite all the setbacks, De Lorean Motor Company rolled out its first vehicles in May 1981, only eight months behind schedule. The cars started out selling fairly well in the United States—which had always been the target market, as the left-side-positioned steering wheel attested. The British government nixed De Lorean's request for $70 million in export credits to keep shipping product, instead assigning an accounting agency to vet DMC's books. Finding the company to be technically insolvent, they placed it in receivership—and thereby bought De Lorean some time to scramble for an angel.

What De Lorean came up with was no angel or a knight—but it *was* white. He was busted in Los Angeles with 60 pounds of cocaine on November 11, 1982, thus ending his saga with an especially ignominious exclamation mark. De Lorean claimed that he hadn't known the nature of the deal he was involved in, and the court apparently believed him. De Lorean was acquitted on all counts, but his reputation was shattered and his dream, of course, was, too.

The actual mistakes he made fall into two categories: managerial and financial. On the first front, he refused to abide by his marketing department's projections of selling no more than 12,000 De Loreans a year; he insisted on shooting for 20,000, and pushed his assembly facility to the max without the necessary marketing, sales, and distribution resources to justify that amplitude of production. As for the financial problems, they boiled down to insufficient capitalization. As much money as he had succeeded in gathering—expending most of his vast reservoir of energy in doing so—it still wasn't enough. At GM, De Lorean had money cascade through bureaucratic channels incapable of converting cash into quality product, and he was convinced that a more efficient operation could achieve cutting-edge greatness with far less. He was right, but he overestimated the degree. Of course, both these errors have a common imprint: arrogance. De Lorean had ample reason for pride or even bluster, but a dollop of humility might have made a big difference. Opting to "work the angles" of the Northern Irish conflict, he's fortunate to have gotten out as intact as he was.

Finally, De Lorean was unlucky: as his first cars rolled out in the early 1980s, the American auto business hit the skids, suffering its worst recession in 50 years. There's only so much pent-up demand for a $26,000 novelty in the best of times, and the De Loreans hit when an opposite climate prevailed.

AFTER
It All

Many extreme entrepreneurs believe their efforts are a part of a Big Picture, something that transcends the accumulation of wealth and prestige, and is greater than just their contribution as business innovators. They are fulfilled by the work, they are pleased by the accomplishment, they enjoy the fruits of their labor. But some see their efforts as a kind of destiny fulfilled, a purposeful contribution to the greater good.

Successful EEs often assert that the quest for personal wealth is not a primary motivator, and is not the guage they use to measure their own success. As one entrepreneur said, "Anyone can make money. But not just anyone can contribute something with real value, something memorable and meaningful, something that lasts."

This isn't to say that every entrepreneur has got some altruistic, higher calling in mind when they set out to make their mark. Often, innovation is driven by a belief, and success happens to follow. Other times, success comes, and a belief system evolves after the fact.

chapter

This chapter looks at some EEs whose efforts and enthusiasms, as well as end results, go beyond the bottom line.

That Old Time Religion

Some people believe Milton Hershey deserves to be sainted, and not just because of what he did for generations of chocolate lovers. Hershey was a shrewd businessman, doggedly determined and with an intense curiosity that fueled a lifetime of manufacturing and product innovation. He was said to have had a genius for timing and a knack for choosing capable, loyal people who enabled him to fulfill his entrepreneurial vision. As if all that wasn't extreme enough, he single-handedly developed the ways and means of mass producing milk chocolate. Like I said, he was a saint.

If you look beyond the vast mountain of chocolate products Milton Hershey shared with the world, you will see a man who probably considered his most meaningful contribution to be civic. Not one to go around talking about his philosophy, he just lived it and let his actions speak for themselves. Besides the business he brought back to his hometown when he established his vast manufacturing plant there, Hershey made a point to encourage business development beyond the walls of the chocolate factory. Even during the darkest hours of the Depression, he kept the entire town employed constructing a hotel, an office building, and other community buildings. He believed in his own moral obligation to share his success with others, and went the extra mile in establishing the Hershey Industrial School, an institution through which he felt his fortune could make a difference.

> Milton Hershey was fiercely committed to his vision as an entrepreneur, but he was equally committed to his standards of integrity, fairness, and quality.

Milton Hershey was fiercely committed to his vision as an entrepreneur, but he was equally committed to his standards of integrity, fairness,

EE Superstar: Levi Strauss

In 1853, Bavarian immigrant Levi Strauss settled in San Francisco, where he planned to open a dry goods business like the one owned by his brothers in New York. He built a thriving business, and by 1873 he had patented the process of using rivets in work pants for strength (a tailor to whom Strauss sold cloth approached him with the idea, which Strauss was smart enough to bankroll), and Levi's jeans were born. They called them "waist overalls" then, and we call them a multi-billion dollar great idea now.

Strauss himself had a reputation for commitment to his employees and to his community, and devoted lots of time to charitable activities. His company also had a long history of corporate responsibility. After the San Francisco earthquake of 1906, the company placed newspaper ads alerting employees that they still had jobs, even if there was, for the moment, no place to work. Fast forward to the 1960s, when Levi Strauss & Co. was a leading advocate of integration and aggressive minority hiring. They've likewise taken a lead in AIDS education, discrimination, and youth issues, with a foundation that funds programs in more than 40 countries to the tune of more than $16 million a year.

> Strauss himself had a reputation for commitment to his employees and to his community, and devoted lots of time to charitable activities.

The company has won awards for outstanding achievement in employee and community relations, and founded a groundbreaking employee volunteer initiative that warranted a White House honor. Even though the company came under criticism when it took some manufacturing outside the country in the '80s, and has stumbled through some significant management shifts, it still stands tall as a standard bearer for corporate responsibility. Current COO Robert Haas has said, "It's really important to be clear about what your values are. People tend to respond more strongly to values they agree with." Thanks to Strauss's early, simple acts of kindness and charity, the company has grown into a model for corporate citizenship.

and quality. The fruit of his convictions is alive and well today in the legacy of his efforts—his company, his community, and his school.

It Takes a Village

For Candice Carpenter, the road to her big contribution was circuitous. Armed with degrees from Stanford and Harvard Business School, Carpenter had all the fixings for a fast-track shot up the ladder. Indeed, before founding iVillage in 1995, Carpenter was president of Q2, the cable shopping channel, as well as of Time-Life Video and Television. It was her experience as a part-time consultant for AOL that led her to her epiphany, both as an entrepreneur and as an individual.

"I was a new mom…and when I went online I saw that most of the programming on the Internet was for men," Carpenter has said. "But I also noticed that there were places with enormous interaction between women. My idea was to connect women with each other." It was a nice enough idea, and certainly a viable premise for an Internet business venture (or any entrepreneurial venture, for that matter)—you see a niche, you fill it. Indeed, by 2000, iVillage had become the leading online destination for women, a community site featuring 14 channels covering family, health, work, personal finance, and more. With over four million members and 52 million page views per month, iVillage has more than actualized Carpenter's vision.

But what she has really discovered on her winding way to the Internet revolution (and her subsequent blockbuster IPO in 1999), is that her real contribution—and measure of her own success—was in creating value. She sees this as her own most meaningful accomplishment, as well as the goal she urges on all the women and entrepreneurs her efforts have inspired. As Carpenter told *Fast Company* in 1997, "If you are committed to creating value, and if you aren't afraid of the hard times, obstacles become utterly unimportant. A nuisance, perhaps, but with no real power. The world respects creation."

Insurance industry iconoclast Bob MacDonald concurs, and takes the concept one step further by putting his money where the value is. "If people have the ability to create value, they will be encouraged to do so if they get to share in the value created. This is a very simple yet revolutionary statement in corporate America." So MacDonald makes sure his people at LifeUSA share in the value they've created by pursuing an aggressive ownership approach: employees and agents own substantial stock in the company, which has produced a tangible, positive sense of community in the ranks. The better they perform as employees and agents, the more value created for the company, and the more value created for themselves.

We Are Family

Some of the most notable family ventures in business history look more like train wrecks than entrepreneurial endeavors. Think of the bickering Binghams or the scuffling Schlitzes, to name just a couple. But what of the non-family ventures whose most compelling feature is how much the whole thing feels like, well, family?

More than offering just good pay and benefits, the best operations have figured out what combination of workplace policy, corporate culture, and meaningful compensation makes it worth the while of employees to go along for the entrepreneur's wild ride. To these motivated employees, work isn't just better than a sharp stick in the eye. Their work-life experience is meaningful, their efforts are appreciated, and they feel they've been an important part of the venture. For some founding entrepreneurs, this contribution is legacy enough.

> Some of the most notable family ventures in business history look more like train wrecks than entrepreneurial endeavors.

Companies like Herb Kelleher's Southwest Airlines, Charles Schwab, Qualcomm, and Cisco Systems are creating employment opportunities and corporate cultures that have more than responded to the needs of a changing workforce. By thinking hard about what it takes to recruit and keep the best employees, and what it takes to make them feel they have a stake in the company's success, the EEs that forged these companies are blazing trails and carving legacies that the rest of corporate America is going to have trouble living up to. They are progressive, standard-setting ventures that understand that by being flexible and responsive, they are helping employees balance their home and work lives. While these companies and their founders may be remembered by history as fabulous

After It All

195

The New Philanthropy

In 1997, Ted Turner's bold gift of $1 billion dollars to establish a new foundation in support of the United Nations upped the ante on big giving. Many considered this an uppity gesture meant to poke the ribs of the old rich to the point of discomfort for their relative stinginess. Maybe so. But it was also a gesture that challenged the new, entrepreneurial rich to think about how to give back.

Cisco Systems founders Leonard Bosack and Sandy Lerner created the Bosack/Kruger Foundation in 1990, endowing it with $34 million for animal welfare. In total, the pair have donated nearly 75 percent of their Cisco fortunes ($112 million) for charitable purposes.

Others are sticking close to home, sending money back to the schools that prepared them for the entrepreneurial world. Intel founder Gordon Moore has given millions to UC Berkeley and California Institute of Technology. Yahoo!'s David Filo and Jerry Yang endowed a $2 million chair at alma mater Stanford.

I know I wasn't going to talk about the usual suspects in this book, and Bill Gates is Usual Suspect #1. But we can't discuss legacy without having a quick look at what the Microsoft founder and chairman has been up to, philanthropically speaking. Bill and Melinda Gates have endowed a foundation with more than $17 billion to support a wide range of global philanthropic programs. The foundation supports the Gates Library Initiative, which intends to bring computers, Internet access, and computer training to public libraries. Of course, it doesn't hurt that he might be growing future Microsoft customers in the process.

entrepreneurial endeavors that generated immeasurable wealth and value, they may be remembered by employees as much more.

Making Good, Then Doing Good

No one can argue with Charles Schwab's success story—he founded the nation's first and largest discount brokerage firm, which, since going public in 1987, has reached a market valuation of more than $23 billion. And no one can say Schwab is not extreme—an entrepreneurial soul since childhood, he took his knack for economics and turned it into the most profitable financial endeavor since the advent of modern banking. He got where he was going the hard way, having suffered his entire life from serious dyslexia.

His lifelong struggle with this learning disability forced Schwab to rely on his other strengths, which included good communication skills, an aptitude for quantitative and technical subjects, and a good-sized dash of charm. He pushed his way through high school and college, which he described as "a crushing time" due to his learning challenge. He moved quickly on to finance, and ten years later borrowed $100,000 from his uncle and founded the brokerage firm that bears his name.

He never understood the nature of his own problem until his son was diagnosed with dyslexia many years later. Once he became aware of the condition, he made it his mission to provide help for children with this affliction. In 1990, Schwab put his wealth and marketing genius to work and launched the Schwab Foundation for Learning, a nonprofit that provides information and guidance to parents and teachers of children with learning differences, from dyslexia to attention deficit disorders. Schwab is passionate about the Foundation's work, and points to the fact that kids with learning problems are twice as likely to drop out of school or end up in trouble with the law. "If we don't handle these things right," he has said, "it's a real problem for society."

World Changers

Many EEs see their work and their products or services as a fundamental advance in the world. Steve Jobs has always had an exalted sense of mission associated with the advent of the personal computer. Along with Mitch Kapor and hundreds of other important contributors to the microcomputer, software, and Internet fields, Jobs was highly influenced by the mystical hippie perspective. Stewart Brand, writer, thinker, and intellectual avatar of this visionary flank, has written about this uncommon strand of experimental entrepreneurship that runs through both the back-to-the-land and the techno-utopian arms of the 1960s-derived counterculture. Certainly, Paul Hawken,

> Many EEs see their work and their products or services as a fundamental advance in the world.

whose Erewhorn Company was instrumental in launching the multi-billion-dollar natural foods industry, is a fine representative of this crossover.

In the more meat-and-potatoes domain, there are people such as Fred Smith, who always considered FedEx a critical component in the evolving technocratic society. In his eyes, the delivery service has been a linchpin in ensuring that computer parts, in particular, can be quickly replaced. Smith, a Vietnam War veteran, understood that computers were to be the crucial engine driving business into its next phase, and he's been gratified to have facilitated that transition.

Steel and the Common Weal

The term "giveback" was unknown in the early 20th century, but the concept was alive and well.

Andrew Carnegie is one of the great representatives of the socially generous EE. Part of what makes him such is the complexity of his temperament. Raised in abject poverty in Scotland, Carnegie paid verbal testament to the plight of the poor throughout his career and to the humane treatment of labor. In the latter regard, however, his vision fell far short of his rhetoric, as he resisted workers' rights much more than he promoted them. For example, he failed to see that wages should be based on productivity, not steel prices, and that a workweek comprising seven days of 12-hour shifts was brutal and antiquated.

> Andrew Carnegie is one of the great representatives of the socially generous EE.

But probably the most heinous thing associated with Carneige was the horrific Homestead incident of 1892, one of the definitive battles between American capital and labor, in which 14 men were killed and over 160 wounded. While the debacle is often blamed on unilateral decisions of his CEO Henry Frick, Carnegie knew he bore ultimate responsibility. He was deeply anguished by the bloodshed—and the taint upon his reputation.

Although Carnegie certainly questioned the worthiness of devoting one's life to accruing wealth, his brilliance at business and competitive streak kept him at it for most of his life. At 33, he'd asserted that, "To continue…with most of my thoughts wholly upon the way to make more money in the shortest time must degrade me beyond hope of permanent recovery." Perhaps this Hamlet-like streak of ambivalence owed something to Carnegie's love of poetry—which he often quoted—and his claim that Shakespeare was one of the very few men who'd understood human nature better than he himself did.

Carnegie's puckish delight in business and Falstaffian gusto obviously trumped any misgivings. Colossal EE that he was, there was no way to stifle his entrepreneurial will. Plus, Carnegie well knew his steel empire was more than a means for him to attain vast wealth; it was the very ground on which industrialization and technical progress was able to proceed.

In Carnegie's last two decades of life, he finally realized lofty, nonbusiness ambitions. As he asserted in his book, *The Gospel of Wealth*, "A rich man dies honorably only if he dies poor"—that is, having carefully given away as much of his acquired wealth as possible. Carnegie walked his talk. Of $300 million he'd amassed by the time he sold U.S. Steel and retired from business in 1902, Carnegie gave away all but $30 million—which he left to his wife and daughter.

Carnegie left as much of a mark with his philanthropic work as he did in business, and his legacy to the world was both vast and deep. Among his contributions were the following:

○ New York's Carnegie Hall

○ Museums and institutes of art and music in Pittsburgh and Washington

○ Pittsburgh's Carnegie Institute of Technology (which later became Carnegie-Mellon)

○ The Carnegie Foundation, Carnegie Trusts for the Advancement of Teaching and for the Universities of Scotland

○ The Peace Palace in The Hague

○ Bequeathal of 4,000 church organs

Carnegie's single greatest achievement, however, was in financing over 3,000 public libraries throughout America and Britain. The creation of a free public library system—one of our society's most democratic and uplifting institutions—was his single-handed doing.

Another philanthropic giant was John D. Rockefeller—the man who built Standard Oil Trust, which dominated the U.S. oil industry (and engendered controversy, opposition, and animosity along the way). Like Carnegie, Rockefeller aspired to donate the largest possible portion of his vast personal wealth before he died—and like Carnegie, he succeeded in large measure.

Rockefeller personally contributed greatly to churches and African-American education. He was the primary source of financing behind the University of Chicago. And he pioneered the institution of "corporate philanthropy"—a charitable corporation given title to a huge fund of capital and overseen by trustees and officers with specialized training.

Rockefeller's most revolutionary move was to drastically improve the country's medical research structure and health standards. Through his Rockefeller Institute for Medical Research, the Rockefeller Sanitary Commission, and numerous specific programs, he made huge strides to upgrade a medical system still shamefully subpar. The Rockefeller Foundation expanded this work on a worldwide scale, creating basic structures of public health services and aggressively working to control and eliminate diseases such as hookworm, malaria, and yellow fever.

Going, Going, Gone

Fast forward a hundred years or so and you'll see very clearly how much the notion of giveback has morphed. Pierre Omidyar, the founder of online auction megasite eBay, is a thoroughly modern, first-class extreme entrepreneur. He also has a very distinctive outlook that is simple and revolutionary—and may in the end have more lasting value than his billions.

Omidyar didn't set out to become a billionaire or to change the world—he was just a technogeek who gravitated to Silicon Valley during its wildest West period. He was immediately struck by how the financial markets were arbitrarily skewing the fate of Internet start-ups. Omidyar found that the financial institutions and large investors had all the information and influence, and he wondered whether it was possible to create a marketplace where everyone was equally vested and had access to the same information.

The first truth Omidyar observed as he began to forge this democratic vision was that the Internet was a vehicle for large companies to peddle more stuff to consumers. He saw this as a negative—and an opportunity for individuals to wedge themselves into the market dynamic, to establish their own collective power together as producers in the marketplace.

From this notion came eBay's most powerful weapon in the battle for market domination—community. The we're-a-bunch-of-little-guys-in-this-together factor *is* the e-Bay community—eBay sellers see themselves as a likeminded throng of entrepreneurs—and is its most valuable resource.

Pierre Omidyar also felt a deep sense of duty as the founder of eBay to imbue the culture with his values. As a company whose business is comprised of the efforts of millions of complete strangers, this is no small task. Omidyar has said: "My mother always taught me to treat other people the way I wanted to be treated and to have respect for other people. Those are just good basic values to have in a crowded world." Not just good values, but good business, as eBay depends almost entirely on the quality of the relationships between buyers and sellers. While eBay knows it cannot legislate the way users behave toward one another, it has managed to encourage the community to play nice, to adopt a set of values that enables a favorable, profitable eBay experience.

We live in litigious times, and consumer fraud is more sophisticated than ever, but eBay has successfully (and improbably, some might argue) employed the honor code to grease the wheels of commerce on the site. Sellers must be honest about what they're selling and ultimately delivering to buyers, and buyers must be honest about timely payment to sellers. If not, then they are asked to leave the eBay community.

Funny that it basically boils down to the Golden Rule for eBay. Pierre Omidyar would be happy if this were his legacy, having enabled the creation of a community where people are empowered and encourage each other to be the best they can be as entrepreneurs, consumers, and partners in the game of buying and selling. Omidyar has left eBay's day-to-day management in the eminently capable hands of CEO Meg Whitman, and has moved to Paris to work on eBay's international plans for expansion and to develop a charitable foundation, which, like eBay itself, is based on encouraging values and civility in a "crowded world."

• • •

As in all the preceding chapters, what should be obvious is that EEs measure success in terms radically divergent from conventional thinking. Whereas even exceptional entrepreneurs would be more than gratified to create a highly profitable business and well-run organization, and *then* pursue socially engaged glory in their retirement, that's not the EE way. Our breed of subjects wants to move and change the world *through* their works, rather than relegate this mission to their golden years.

INDEX

Volvo, 122–123

W

Wal-Mart, 17
Walker, Jay, 144–145. *See also* price-line.com
Walker, Madame C. J., 86, 88, 141–143
Walton, Sam, 17. *See also* Wal-Mart
Waterman, Robert, 162, 171. *See also* Peters, Tom
Watson, Thomas Sr., 140–141. *See also* IBM
Web, 21–22. *See also* Internet
Web business, 77–78
Web pioneers, 113
Web-based marketing, 114
Weill, Sanford, 168. *See also* Citigroup
Weyerhauser, 70–72
Whitman, Meg, 152. *See also* eBay
Winfrey, Oprah, 10
wired world, 103–104
woman-owned businesses, 95
women entrepreneurs, 23
women's clothing designer. *See* Fisher, Eileen
work-centrism, 7–8
Wozniak, Steve, 56. *See also* Apple Computer
Wrigley, 111–112, 136–137
Wrigley, William Jr., 6, 111–112, 136–137

X

X.com, 35
Xerox, 67

Y

Yahoo!, 56–58, 65–66
  hiring, 151–152
Yang, Jerry, 56–58. *See also* Yahoo!
Yoyodyne, 159